Connect with Charlotte

Email: charlottevivolife@gmail.com

Substack: https://charlotteesm.substack.com/

Instagram: @_charlotte_esme_

Your life is a sacred dance, with your key relationships pointing you towards the steps you must take to fall into an embodiment of love, as you respond to the music, cadence, and sacred rhythm of love, you will know intuitively what is required of you, where your growth points are, and what steps you need to master to be the love you seek.

*Celebrate the sacredness of*
*your relationship*

Relationships are our greatest spiritual assignments.

If you could create the relationship and lifestyle you have secretly dreamed about and yearned for, would you?

If you knew, without a shadow of a doubt that it is possible, would you be willing to move beyond the familiar shores of your mind and your current experiences and embrace the unknown?

# CONTENTS

# THE PRACTICES INDEX

# Welcome to Spiritual Seduction

The transformational and Spiritual Nature of Relationships

Welcome to Spiritual Seduction, a little book of intimacy for couples that will take you on a journey of discovering the depths of your relationship. This book is not just about sex or physical intimacy, although these aspects of your relationship will benefit from the practices. The book delves into the spiritual and emotional aspects of your partnership.

Intimacy is a crucial component of any relationship, but it can be challenging to maintain and nourish over time. In today's fast-paced world, where technology and distractions are commonplace, it's more important than ever before to cultivate a deeper connection with your partner.

This book will guide you through practical tools, exercises, and practices that will help you tap into your innermost desires and needs. You will learn how to communicate more effectively, connect on a deeper level, and reignite the spark of passion that may have been lost along the way.

Whether you are a new couple or have been together for years, this book will offer valuable insights and practical tools to help you enhance your relationship and experience greater intimacy. Let's embark on this journey together and discover the power of spiritual seduction in your love life.

I believe relationships have the potential to be transformative and spiritual experiences. When two people come together in a relationship, they bring their unique histories, personalities, and values, thus creating opportunities for immense growth and learning.

One way that relationships can be transformative is by providing a mirror for our behaviour and beliefs. As we interact with our partners, we may become more aware of our strengths and weaknesses, patterns of behaviour, and areas for growth. This self-awareness can lead to personal transformation and personal development.

Relationships can also be spiritual in nature. When two people connect deeply and authentically, they may experience a sense of transcendence or oneness with the universe. This can lead to a greater purpose and meaning in life. The relationship can be dedicated to a life of service to one another and a motivating force to awaken into a wholesome, well-rounded and conscious human being. Moreover, relationships can provide a supportive environment for spiritual practices and self-development. Couples may find that practising meditation, breathwork, intentional living, or conscious communication enhances their sense of connectedness and intimacy.

However, it's important to note that not all relationships are transformative or spiritual. It takes intention, effort, and a willingness to be vulnerable and open to create a conscious connection. Additionally, it is vital to ensure that the relationship is healthy and respectful, as a toxic relationship or one where we are indifferent to showing up as our fullest expression can hinder personal growth and spiritual development.

There are many forms of relationship with equally many reasons for entering into one. Within our intimate relationship with our chosen other, it is helpful to discover the motivating forces behind our choice and the purpose that the relationship affords us. We may consider our relationship to be a unified path of purpose. One that is consciously chosen and committed to. The flavour and divine purpose of our relationships may change at different stages in our lives and personal development as a reflection of our core values, needs, and unique expressions of love.

When we understand that each relationship houses three energetic entities—our own, our partners, and the relationship itself, we may be more willing to look at how we show up and express ourselves, thus co-creating with the other—consciously and unconsciously. These three unique and intimately entwined energetic fields influence and inform the other and may, if we so choose, serve our own, each other and the relational growth.

I belive relationships can be a significant source of personal growth and spiritual development. Within the sacred container of the relationship, we are gifted opportunities to learn about ourselves, cultivate powerful qualities such as empathy and compassion, and deepen our understanding of the human experience. Relationships can also challenge us in profound ways as they reveal our strengths and weaknesses and move us to confront our fears and insecurities. As we navigate the complexities of human connection, we may be called upon to develop qualities such as patience, forgiveness, and acceptance.

In addition to personal growth, relationships may provide us with opportunities to serve others and contribute to the greater good. When we approach relationships with compassion and generosity, we may create meaningful connections that powerfully transform our lives and the lives of those around us.

As we embrace relational challenges as opportunities for growth, we may deepen our connection to each other and support one another in individual, relational, and spiritual growth. Our relationships are beautiful vehicles towards self-actualisation as we deepen our understanding of ourselves and the world around us and ultimately lead more fulfilling lives.

**Relationships are our greatest spiritual assignments.**

When you ignite your potential as a couple and redefine relational intimacy, you will take your relationship and life to the next level. This is sacred soul work and vital for a thriving life beyond the honeymoon period.

If you aspire to become the couple you dreamed of at the beginning of your relationship by co-creating your relationship on your terms and keeping the spark alive by transforming unhelpful patterns of putting your relationship last on the list of priorities and coming back to the centre together, united as you intended right from the start, the practices within this book will help you.

It's not too late to reignite the spark of attraction, closeness, and a dual commitment to creating a private life of ease, joy, and connection again by exploring polarity, the play of love, and resting in oneness.

Are you ready to develop skills to nurture your relationship and clear all that holds you back from creating all you desire?

If not now, when?

Draw a line in the sand between what was and who you are, in becoming—united in love and with a clear and unwavering commitment to go all in together.

It's time to redefine what you thought was possible.

This book is a guide to simple yet powerful practices to help you connect with your partner on a deeper level as you reawaken the passion you once shared or create a strong foundation for the duration of your relationship. These practices will aid you in creating a relational dynamic where your desire for greater love, connection, and intimacy is upheld and supported.

# NURTURING YOUR RELATIONSHIP: A PATH TO WHOLESOME AUTHENTICITY

*As you dedicate yourself and your relationship to deepening, evolving, and supporting one another in showing up as the best version of yourself, these practices will support you in fostering a deeper emotional connection and ever-enriching intimacy, while growing your connection with one another.*

In your quest to nurture your relationship and foster personal growth, it is essential to honour the intelligence of your heart. By choosing self-enrichment and growing your capacity for intimacy, connection, and individual development, you can create thriving relationships with yourself and others. Moreover, this growth extends to nourishing your children and deepening your connection to the diverse beauty of life.

As an individual, couple, and family, you must transcend the boundaries of closure, fear, and emotional withholding. By doing so, you create a metaphorical 'Heaven on Earth' within the sacred container of your home. As you awaken and recognise the sacredness in all circumstances, this initiates a collective transformation that transcends your limitations. This transformational journey radiates outward, enriching the lives of friends, family, and your broader communities.

On a global scale, the responsibility for change rests with each of us. There is an invitation to take ownership of how we present ourselves, causing our collective consciousness to expand exponentially. This shift leads to a paradigm of unity, mutual love, respect, and boundless potential. It all begins within ourselves and the sacred container of relationships we co-create. The ripple effect of our expanded capacity for love extends in ever-widening waves, touching lives beyond our wildest dreams.

Choosing to thrive within the soulful connection of your relationship invites you to delve deeper within and embody the change you aspire to see in the world. The most vital relationship we cultivate is with yourself. All other relationships reflect who you are and how you exist, given that we live in a relational, relative reality.

*Choose love and love will choose you.*

By transforming your relationship with yourself, naturally, all other relationships that emanate from you will shift, too. This process involves a soulful connection with your deepest desires, casting aside the binds of the past, and consciously crafting a new self-identity. This new sense of self magnetically attracts people, places, and circumstances aligned with your evolving self-concept.

Embrace an ongoing evolution within yourself to effectively create change in the world by assuming responsibility for your existence instead of blaming external circumstances. Your self-imposed limitations and conditioning collectively shape the stories you live. By committing to your inner exploration and self-transformation, your lived reality will shift as a mirror to your deepening connection with yourself.

Fundamentally, life is all about relationships with your loved ones playing a pivotal role in helping you to understand yourself more intimately as they reflect your internal beliefs about yourself, others, and the world. Your heart's intelligence discerns the rights and wrongs as it unveils sacred truths that may inspire you to navigate your life's journey with conscious awareness.

When faced with relationship challenges, see them as opportunities for growth. Embrace your triggers and the frictions you encounter, for they serve as sacred gateways to a life filled with love, beauty, and connection. As you allow your energetic heart's intuitive wisdom to guide you through challenging moments, you will be shown the way forward. Living consciously with an open heart and an open mind, led by your soul, encourages you to approach life with a YES and MORE PLEASE attitude. This mindset will guide you to experience expansion from within.

Paying attention to the subtle signals of your body's intelligence, breathing patterns, and gut instincts, you have an internal guide to lead you on your path with greater ease and attuned self-awareness. As you tune in and listen to the wisdom of your innermost being, you gain the power to take inspired, deliberate actions towards embodying your Highest Self. By honouring these internal signals, you chart your course deliberately whilst remaining aligned with your integrity.

Throughout my relational history and experiences as a daughter, partner, wife, parent, teacher,

*When we let Love live our life, we allow the
flow of Grace to envelop us in All ways as
we live with radiant presence, trust, and
an intimate connection to All that Is.*

and more, I discovered the importance of healthy and honest communication in relationships. Without this foundation, we cannot achieve true intimacy and a strong connection with our partner and loved ones. Through practice, I've learned to trust my inner wisdom and recognise the signals that guide me, leading me to a path of deeper self-understanding and connection to my emotional, sensual and sensitive self. By embracing this path of inner knowing and clear communication, you can discover what resonates with you and reveal aspects of yourself that you may have suppressed or otherwise ignored.

Sharing these inner reflections and this greater self-understanding with your beloved can deepen your connection as you grow and evolve with trust, sensitivity and courage. It may seem challenging to prioritise your relationship, given your many commitments. This path of relational intimacy is for the highest good of all. By supporting each other in becoming the best versions of yourselves, you will inspire greater love, commitment and curiosity as you individually and collectively pursue your dreams and live your truth.

Embrace your journey of becoming, listening to the innate wisdom within you as you evolve through your relationships with others. This path leads you to a life of authenticity, wholeness, and boundless love.

I am still working towards living each moment of my life this way and invite you to embrace this calling, too. Due to the busyness of this modern and evolving world and the culture we live in, along with the numerous responsibilities each of us faces, it may seem challenging to be that present with ourselves and others, leading us to de-prioritise our relationships. I encourage you to explore this path wholeheartedly.

It is important to remember that you and your partner came together for a reason. There is a relational 'why'. Therefore, it is your responsibility to be committed to this why and discover what is needed from you in your relationship. As you support one another in becoming the best version of

*The most important relationship we will ever cultivate is with ourselves.*

your unique selves, you will both rise in consciousness, becoming an inspiration to others as you embody greater love, commitment, and curiosity as you create your living dream and cast aside all that is out of integrity with your truth.

You are in the process of becoming through the interaction of yourself in a relationship with others. In knowing yourself through the other, you will experience—if you are willing to do the work—a blossoming up and outwards of your truth in being.

# WHO CAN BENEFIT FROM THIS BOOK

 *This book has been created with you at the heart of it. It provides you with tools, insights, and guidance to support you in expanding beyond your current relational dynamics and nurturing a depth of intimacy and greater connection with your loved ones.*

There are many reasons you may have chosen to pick up this book at this specific time in your life. Perhaps you are in a long-term relationship and feeling a little stuck or uninspired by your and your partner's current dynamics, finding yourself ready to rekindle the spark of interest, curiosity, and passion as you aim and reconnect with your lover on a deeper level. Perhaps you are in a new relationship and would love to have some beautiful practices and ways of relating to explore as you embrace a vision for your future together. You may be in between relationships and wishing to embody a new way of being when you are ready to engage in intimacy with a new committed partnership.

Perhaps you have experienced past relational challenges or are currently having various issues as a couple and are not ready to release the relationship. While the specific issues can vary from one couple to another, some common problems that might have led you here to explore this book are:

## Lack of Emotional Intimacy
Many couples struggle with emotional intimacy, feeling disconnected or emotionally distant from their partners. You may want to deepen your emotional connection and vulnerability in the relationship.

## Communication Problems
Poor communication can lead to misunderstandings, conflicts, and feelings of being unheard. You may seek help improving your communication skills and understanding each other better.

## Waning of Passion and Romance

Over time, the passion and romantic spark in a relationship can dwindle. You might want to reignite your physical and emotional connection.

## Trust Issues
Trust is fundamental in a relationship, and if it has been damaged due to infidelity, betrayal, or other reasons it is beneficial to have support, practices, and an intention to rebuild your relational foundations. You may want to work on rebuilding trust.

## Spiritual or Energetic Disconnect
Some couples might feel a lack of spiritual or energetic connection in their relationship. You may seek ways to explore and strengthen this aspect of your connection.

## Monotony and Routine
Couples may find that their relationship has become routine or monotonous. You might be looking for ways to bring novelty and excitement back into your lives.

## Stress and Life Changes
Life events, such as major transitions, job changes, or the arrival of children can strain a relationship.
You may need help in navigating these changes and maintaining your connection.

## Conflict Resolution
Frequent or unresolved conflicts can put a strain on a relationship. You may be ready to embrace guidance on effective conflict resolution techniques.

## Long-Term Relationship Maintenance
Maintaining a healthy and fulfilling long-term relationship requires effort and attention. You might be looking for resources to keep your relationship strong.

## Desire for Deeper Connection
Regardless of the specific issues, you may desire to deepen your connection and enhance your overall intimacy on both emotional and energetic levels.

However, it's important to remember that no single book or resource can solve all relationship problems. You may also benefit from relationship coaching, therapy, or seeking guidance from relationship experts to address your unique challenges.

This book offers practical tools and insights to cultivate conscious emotional and energetic intimacy, enrich your relationship, and deepen your connections.

# BECOMING CLEAR:
# KNOWING THY SELF

*The key to relational success is self awareness.*

The journey toward greater self-awareness and understanding invites a deliberate commitment to gain clarity about oneself. By engaging in introspection and fostering self-awareness with a curious and compassionate heart, you delve deeper into your values, beliefs, desires, strengths, weaknesses, and motivations, thus unravelling a profound understanding of your authentic self. This is a gift to yourself and your loved ones. The greater your self-understanding is, the more you are able and willing to show up for others with curiosity and presence without shying away from your or their truth.

This set of relationship journaling prompts is designed to assist you in evaluating your relationship, delving into your interpersonal dynamics, and your relationship-related needs. It is essential to be genuinely open and radically honest with yourself during this process, as it is within the unfiltered truth that you discover invaluable wisdom. If you both feel inclined, you and your partner may also consider sharing your reflections. If you opt to do this, be patient, and understanding and practice compassionate non-judgment towards your partner.

## Journal Prompts: Know Thy Self
1. What initially attracted you to your current partner or the person you're interested in?
2. Reflect on your communication style with your partner. What are your strengths and weaknesses in this area?
3. Describe a recent conflict in your relationship. How did you handle it, and how could you improve your conflict resolution skills?
4. What are the top three values or priorities you believe are crucial in a successful relationship?
5. How do you express love and affection in your relationship, and how would you like to

improve in this regard?

6. Consider your past relationships. What patterns or themes do you notice in your romantic history?

7. Reflect on your emotional availability in your current relationship. Are there any emotional barriers you need to address?

8. List five things that make you feel appreciated and loved in a relationship. How can you communicate these to your partner?

9. Describe your ideal date night or quality time with your partner. How often do you make time for this?

10. What role does trust play in your relationship, and how can it be strengthened or repaired if necessary?

11. Think about your support system outside of your relationship. How do your friends and family view your partner, and how does this impact your relationship?

12. Consider your long-term goals and aspirations. How do they align with your partner's, and how can you work together to achieve them?

13. Reflect on any insecurities or self-doubts that affect your relationship. How can you address and overcome them?

14. Describe the role of intimacy in your relationship. Are your physical and emotional needs being met?

15. Think about the ways you and your partner handle stress and challenges together. What coping strategies work well, and which ones need improvement?

16. Reflect on your boundaries in the relationship. Are there any areas where you need to establish or adjust boundaries?

17. How do you handle disagreements or differences of opinion with your partner? Are there ways to improve your conflict resolution skills?

18. Consider your roles and responsibilities within the relationship. Are they balanced, or do they need adjustment?

19. Reflect on your level of independence and autonomy within the relationship. Do you have the space to pursue your interests and goals?

20. Describe your partner's strengths and qualities that you admire. How often do you express your appreciation for these attributes?

21. Think about the last time you felt truly connected with your partner. What were you doing, and how can you recreate that feeling more often?

22. Reflect on your personal growth within the relationship. In what ways has your partner influenced your growth, and vice versa?

23. Consider the importance of shared experiences and adventures in your relationship. How can you create more memorable moments together?

24. Reflect on the role of compromise in your relationship. Are there areas where you need to find a middle ground more effectively?

25. Describe your ideal vision of a healthy, fulfilling relationship. How does your current

relationship measure up to this vision?

26. Reflect on your ability to forgive and let go of past grievances in your relationship. Are there unresolved issues that need attention?

27. Think about the balance between giving and receiving in your relationship. Are you both contributing equally to its success and happiness?

28. Consider the role of patience and understanding in your relationship. How can you practice these virtues more consistently?

29. Reflect on your future together. What are your shared dreams and goals, and how do you plan to work toward them?

30. Imagine your relationship one year from now. What positive changes and growth would you like to see?

These journaling prompts can help you gain insight into your relationships, foster communication with your partner, and work towards healthier, more fulfilling connections.

# THE PURPOSE OF CONSCIOUS INTIMATE RELATIONSHIPS

*The purpose of conscious intimate relationships is to foster deep and meaningful connections between two individuals, allowing you to grow and evolve together.*

As we reflect upon the essence of conscious intimate relationships, we find ourselves entangled in an awakening process of reverence, respect, and spiritual growth. The sacred bonds we weave are a testament to the power of human connection, a reminder that love can be an alchemical force, transforming our relationships and ourselves, too.

Conscious intimate relationships are unique in their essence, marked by a profound awareness and intentionality that sets them apart from ordinary unions. These relationships are not left to chance or day-to-day circumstances. They are crafted, moulded, and nurtured with care. They are the gardens of the heart, where seeds of trust and vulnerability are sown, and the roots of personal growth and transformation dig deep. Remember that the grass is always greener where we water it.

At the core of conscious intimacy lies the commitment to creating a space of safety and growth. A place where both individuals can fully express themselves. This sacred container of love and connection provides the fertile ground in which we plant the seeds of our true selves. It is a space where we realise that our partner is not just our significant other but a mirror reflecting our inner world.

Every conscious relationship thrives on communication, trust, and respect. Partners continuously dance in vulnerability and authenticity, learning to reveal their deepest fears, hopes, and dreams. In this dance, we confront our emotional burdens and insecurities, face them head-on, and grow stronger together.

Conscious intimate relationships have a unique purpose—to allow both partners to evolve and transform within the sacred cocoon of love. Your invitation is to begin a journey of self-discovery, to explore the vast space between who you are and who you are becoming. This journey is undertaken hand in hand with an unwavering commitment to go all in together.

Consider the alternative—putting off personal growth and neglecting the nurturing of your relationship. What would it cost you to remain stagnant, to let the spark of love and connection dim? To not be the love, connection, intimacy, and transformation you seek? Inaction might cost you the fulfilment of your heart's desires and the evolution of your relationship.

But there is hope. You can reignite the spark of love and intimacy. You can allow the depth of your union to flourish in ways you never thought possible. The key lies not in seeking attributes and qualities in your partner but in fostering those qualities within yourself.

Imagine that you become a living embodiment of all you seek in the other. As you cultivate the qualities you wish to experience in your partner within yourself, you create a magnetic field of attraction, a force that draws love, respect, and spiritual growth towards you. The alchemy of conscious intimate relationships begins with you.

Embark on the path of conscious intimacy with an open heart and a willingness to grow. This is your reminder that you have the power to cast off the binds and limitations of the past, nurture the seeds of transformation and become the love, connection, and intimacy you seek. In doing so, you will enrich your relationships, and cultivate the most profound love affair of all—the one with yourself.

Remember:

Clarify what you truly desire in your relationship and recognise how you currently show up, then commit to doing your inner work to resolve any differences between these two states.
Look to the mirror of your partner to see what is being reflected back to you. Your experience with them is a reflection of your inner workings, beliefs, limitations, and unconscious projections.
Remove all expectations that your partner should please you.
Choose love.

# WHAT'S LOVE GOT TO DO WITH IT?

*When you consciously choose love and allow it to transform you, this becomes a spiritual journey of awakening and your relationship will be a sacred dance of souls, a beautiful and enduring expression of the divine.*

In the realm of conscious relationships, love is the compass that guides you through the labyrinth of intimacy. It's the ever-present force that binds two souls, allowing you to explore the depths of connection and transcend the boundaries of the physical. Love, in its purest form, is not just an emotion. It is a conscious choice, a commitment, and a profound spiritual experience. As you embark on this journey of spiritual seduction within your relationship, it is crucial to understand the role that being a purposeful demonstration of love plays in deepening your connection. Love is not merely a fleeting feeling or a passion that fizzles out with time, it is the very foundation upon which your conscious relationship is built.

### Love is a Conscious Choice.
In the early stages of a relationship, love often feels effortless, like a gentle breeze carrying you along. But as time passes and life's challenges unfold, it becomes evident that love is more than a spontaneous emotion—it's a choice. Conscious couples understand that love is a daily decision, a commitment to nurture, cherish, and support each other, even when the storms of life threaten to pull them apart. To make love a conscious choice in your relationship, practice being present with your partner in both joyful and challenging moments. This allows you to truly see and understand each other.

### Love is a Healing Force
Love has the power to heal wounds, both old and new. In conscious relationships, it becomes a balm for the scars of the past and a source of strength for the future. Through love, you can transform pain into growth and find solace in each other's arms. To harness love as a healing force let go of grudges and resentments. This becomes a gift you give yourself and your partner,

allowing you to move forward with a clean slate. Be a pillar of support during your partner's moments of vulnerability. Empathise with their pain and offer comfort without judgment. Create rituals that symbolise your commitment to transformation together. These can include meditation, energy work, or simply holding each other during difficult times (Refer to and dive into the practices later in this book).

### Accept your partner exactly as they are
Love is about accepting your partner for who they are—flaws and all. Embrace their imperfections as a part of their unique beauty.

### Be the inspiration
To love another deeply, you must be willing to go first, be the inspiration, deal with your triggers as they arise and trust that they want the best for you, as you desire the best for them.

### Build self-respect
Self-respect is the foundation upon which you can build a strong and lasting partnership, with yourself, others, and your intimate partner. Be willing to investigate where you habitually give your power away and disregard your needs.

### Love is a spiritual experience.
In conscious relationships love transcends the mundane and becomes a profound spiritual experience. It is the gateway to a higher state of consciousness where two souls merge and the boundaries of ego dissolve. Love becomes a catalyst for personal and spiritual growth. To experience love on a spiritual level, dive into the practices further on in this book.

### Practice effective communication.
Communication is the bridge that connects hearts and minds. Engage in active listening and open, honest dialogue to maintain a deep connection.

### Rebirth through consciously choosing love.
Ask yourself in each moment of challenge 'What would love have me do and be?' As you move beyond your current limitations and objections, you will emerge stronger, more resilient, and deeply connected.

The transformative power of love can renew your relationship continually. Remember, there are three entities at play within your intimate relationship. There is YOU, the OTHER, and the RELATIONSHIP itself.

Each of these energetic aspects of consciousness are interacting at all times. Your energies blend, polarise and neutralise to various degrees within each moment. This is where having clarity about the purpose of your relationship comes into play so that you may harness it and keep returning to your vision. In this manner, you will energise what you want, essentially learning to ignore what you do not wish to create.

What you focus upon grows and materialises in your environment. You become the living, walking, talking embodiment of your environment as it simultaneously reflects you.

Be conscious of your intentions and be disciplined in holding true to your vision and values in each moment to create what you want. In practice, this will enable you and your partner to thrive in your individuation and within the intimacy of your togetherness.

In the world of conscious relationships, love becomes the response to the question, 'What has love got to do with it?' Love has everything to do with it—it's the cornerstone upon which intimacy is built.

### In Practice:

I've had the privilege of closely supporting couples as they redefine their relationship's purpose once their children have left home. In this period of rediscovery, where they may feel adrift, there is a shared desire to establish a renewed commitment, fostering greater emotional intimacy. This often leads to an exploration of renewed sexual intimacy. Typically, one partner seeks more depth or a change from the habitual nature of their togetherness, and the other is invited along, as they enter the next phase of their life journey together.

# RESISTANCE, FEAR AND BLOCKS TO INTIMACY

*Embrace the beauty of a life well lived in each unfolding moment of your becoming. Rest in oneness, be guided with grace, and surrender to the music of your soul.*

Within the realm of your relationship, it is commonplace to feel charged around conflicts and upsets, resulting in you pointing your finger at the other as the source of your discomfort and suffering. These judgments may help you to shift focus momentarily from yourself and any feelings of confusion, anger, and upset you may be experiencing. This will hold you back from being the love you truly desire. In judging the other, you place your inherent power outside of yourself.

As you deepen your connection to your most genuine self, it will be easier for you to become aware of the circumstances, the triggers—if you will, that cause you to pull back and point the finger and judge others as wrong. Your task, therefore, is to call your power back and take radical responsibility for the circumstances of your relationship. This is a gift to yourself and your loved ones.

Take note of the particular behaviours or qualities displayed by others that you find challenging to hold or bear witness to. In what ways do you also act in the same manner? Are you aware of your matching pattern? Do you disown those parts of yourself and need to condemn another for them? Do you habitually block the experience of suffering rather than assimilate it?

If you allowed yourself to feel and experience your internal resistance and upset, what would change for you? Who would you be? If you find yourself dissociating, avoiding, or dismissing any upset or fear of suffering, what do you hope to achieve by doing so? What does this mean for you long-term? What could be different if you were willing to face and embrace what you habitually turn away from or resist? How do you cope with others' upset? Do you embrace their emotions or turn from them?

Your life is a sacred dance, with your key relationships pointing you towards the steps you must take to fall into an embodiment of love. As you respond to the music, cadence, and sacred rhythm of love, you will know intuitively what is required of you, where your growth points are, and what steps you need to master to be the love you seek.

Your relationships are the training ground for you to open your heart and have it remain open throughout the fluctuations of your life circumstances. This dance of life—of love, moves you beyond yourself to a newfound willingness in your heart to flow, pivot, and course correct as you learn to embrace the desires of your heart.

## Blocks to Intimacy

Blocks to relational intimacy can vary from person to person, but there are some common barriers that many individuals face when trying to connect on a deeper level with others. Here are twelve blocks to relational intimacy and their antidotes:

### Fear or Avoidance of Vulnerability

Practice vulnerability by sharing your thoughts, feelings, and fears with someone you trust. Start with small disclosures and gradually work towards more significant ones. Remind yourself that vulnerability is a sign of strength, not weakness. Trust your partner and allow them to support and understand you.

### Lack of Trust

Build trust gradually through consistent, honest communication and by keeping your promises. Be reliable and demonstrate that you can be counted on.

### Communication Issues

Improve your communication skills by actively listening, asking open-ended questions, and expressing yourself clearly. Schedule times to connect with your partner honestly and openly to discuss important and neglected issues between you.

### Complacency and Apathy

Rekindle your interest in the relationship by exploring new activities, setting shared goals, or seeking novelty. Actively invest time and effort into maintaining, developing, and nurturing the relationship.

### Resentment from Unmet Needs

Address unmet needs by openly communicating your desires with your partner. Seek compromise and work together to meet each other's needs. Practice forgiveness and let go of past resentments. Expectations ruin relationships and lead to heartbreak.

### Past Trauma

Address past traumas through therapy or support groups to heal and prevent them from affecting your current relationships.

### Low Self-Esteem

Work on your self-esteem and self-worth through self-acceptance, self-care, and seeking therapy

---

or coaching if necessary.

## Fear of Rejection

Challenge irrational beliefs about rejection, remember that rejection is a natural part of life, and don't take it personally. Rejection doesn't define your worth and may be considered as a positive redirection towards what you truly desire to experience.

## Defensiveness

Practice active listening, empathy, and a willingness to consider others' perspectives. Let go of the need to be right.

## Poor Boundaries

Learn to set and respect personal boundaries. Communicate about your boundaries clearly and assertively. Be willing to enforce them with loving care when necessary and respectfully honour other people's boundaries, too.

## Fear of Intimacy

Gradually open up to the idea of intimacy by taking small steps towards closeness and building trust over time. Remember that intimacy doesn't have to mean complete emotional exposure all at once.

## Attachment Issues

Seek professional help to address any attachment issues stemming from childhood or past relationships. Develop a better understanding of your attachment style and how it affects your relationships.

These blocks and their corrective measures highlight the importance of proactively engaging in your relationship, addressing resentments, and embracing vulnerability to foster deeper intimacy. Developing a clearer understanding of yourself and your partner's needs and actively working to meet those needs is crucial for building a strong and connected relationship.

This process of self-awareness, relational maturation, and deepening into intimacy is an adventure you embark upon for yourself and bring to the arena of your relationship to both enliven, deepen, and foster greater connection. Remember that your partner does not need fixing. Neither of you is broken.

Working on your blocks to relational intimacy may take time and effort. You may need support from friends, family, a relationship mentor, or a therapist to navigate these challenges, shine a light on your blind spots, and develop a more meaningful and fulfilling connection with others. Be gentle with yourself, and remember you are the love you seek. It is time to dismantle the outdated patterns you have contained yourself to as you shift your identity and embody a new relational paradigm.

# BOUNDARIES ARE SEXY

 *Boundaries are a gift and service to yourself, your loved ones, your life, and your personal connection to that which is Eternally Divine.*

Boundaries are like the essential framework in a relationship—they have masculine undertones. The feminine aspect, on the other hand, interacts and responds to these boundaries. In this dynamic, the feminine establishes its standards and looks for a partner who aligns with those standards by having their core boundaries in place. This interplay is especially evident in your relationships, where you can thoroughly explore the impact of boundaries on your emotional, energetic, and psychological well-being.

When you think about it, boundaries are fascinating spaces for self-discovery, safety, and connection—they are the lines that help you understand where you end and others begin. How do you perceive boundaries—do you embrace them as a way of understanding yourself and fostering deeper connections with the world around you? Or perhaps you find it challenging to establish healthy boundaries?

In reality, boundaries are a natural and integral part of your life. They are meeting points, creating a sacred dance between people, nature, and your inner self. As you acknowledge boundaries as invitations for vulnerable exploration, they challenge you to respond gracefully, whether it involves stepping back or leaning in. These distinctions lie in the space between how you perceive yourself and understand others, guiding you towards greater clarity.

Consider the analogy of a river and its riverbank. They work in harmony, much like the need for boundaries in relationships. Boundaries offer safety and self-discovery, allowing both you and your loved ones to flourish without enmeshment. The riverbank is masculine in structure, whilst the feminine consciousness flows like a river.

Boundaries reflect the quality of your relationships with yourself and others and can ultimately lead to mutual respect and support—as they open avenues for exploration. Are you curious about the spaces in between within your relationships? Do you actively practice energetic awareness to maintain these boundaries? If expressing your boundaries proves difficult, it may be a sign of unmet needs in your life and relationships.

Creating robust, loving boundaries is a means to establish an open and nurturing environment for exploration. Flexibility, honesty, and practice are key to maintaining these boundaries. You may need to reimagine these boundaries as your relationship evolves. Think of a ring as a symbol—it signifies both confinement and an eternal flow, much like the delicate dance between one and the other in relationships. If you have given or received a ring, did you intentionally choose it and the meaning you placed on it? Did you recognise the significance of its symbolic nature?

As you contemplate these symbols of love and connection, honour the importance of upholding your energetic boundaries and living with integrity as you nurture and communicate your sacred boundaries in your closest relationships. If setting boundaries is a struggle due to fear of rejection or neglecting your needs, it is necessary to recognise their importance for flourishing relationships. Let's revisit the analogy of the river—are you an uncertain, chaotic one, do you flow with grace, or are you a well-defined riverbank? By exploring your inner depths, you can provide depth and support to your personal and professional relationships.

Boundaries are intriguing spaces where yin (feminine flow) and yang (masculine direction) meet, resembling the spaces between the brush strokes on a canvas or the gentle touch of a fingertip. They beckon you to explore them emotionally, physically, and energetically. Embrace boundaries as a form of spiritual allure. Value the boundaries of others, extract meaning from their messages, and appreciate the differences and similarities with loving respect.

Let your heart be expansive and wise as you respect yourself and others. By delving into your depths, you can create internal structures that support healthy boundaries in your relationships. Consider boundaries as a gift for both yourself and your relationships. Not held too rigidly but gently porous to allow playful exploration. Recognise those who support you at these boundaries with love, and be brave enough to reveal your needs, thereby finding your inner circle of support.

When you are whole and meet someone with clearly defined boundaries, it becomes an inviting and safe space for celebration and exploration, together. Firm yet flexible boundaries foster respectful intimacy and kindle sensual delight, bringing you closer to yourself and the divine. Your heart is a sacred aspect of yourself, meant for those who respect it, creating a dance of lovers and a gift for self-discovery. Remember, boundaries are not just practical; they are also sexy, offering both love and freedom to your heart.

# THE SACRED ART OF
# COMMUNICATION

*If you desire connection, communicate. Otherwise, you'll keep them guessing and become frustrated that they aren't relating to you in a way that expands your heart.*

When you engage in communication do you go beyond the usual verbal cues, words, body language, and unsaid things? Do you communicate beyond the habit of everyday enquiry, platitudes, and upsets? Are you willing to be bold in your quest to truly understand and be understood rather than coasting along the surface of conversation? It is important to reflect on whether you take communication for granted and assume that others should automatically grasp your desires and intentions without further exploration. Similarly, do you habitually believe you already know the thoughts and needs of the person you're talking to without delving deeper into their perspective and current requirements?

In the realm of healthy communication, it is essential to acknowledge that you filter information through your unique lens, influenced by your thoughts, habits, and beliefs. This means that what you say and what others hear may not always align as you intend. Have you ever considered the possibility that you might not truly know someone beyond the image you have formed of them in your mind? Sometimes, you may project your perceptions onto the energetic space between yourself and others, and they may unknowingly conform to your expectations. The reverse can also happen.

Do you consider communication an art form, a means of both expressing yourself and uncovering new aspects of others? Viewing communication as a means of playful curiosity and understanding, you may practice this art within the context of your relationships. In these interactions, positions and states of consciousness can shift seamlessly when you engage with an open heart and a genuine curiosity about the person in front of you. This interplay between being dominant and submissive, focusing and receiving attention, leading and following, asking questions and receiving questions leads you to discoveries about yourself and others as you deepen intimacy and gain an understanding of each other.

Assuming you know what someone else needs or expecting them to understand your desires can muddy the waters of communication and prevent genuine expressions of love. Expressing your needs lovingly and courageously is your responsibility, allowing your loved ones to choose whether they can meet those needs. Ideally, they should never feel obligated to do so if it doesn't align with their truth. This applies to you as well.

Clear and open communication can prevent misunderstandings and false assumptions. Honest communication leaves space for vulnerable sharing. Exploring each other's communication styles, especially if they are different, will deepen your connection. Be mindful when communicating that others may not fully grasp your message based on their current awareness and understanding.

Commit to understanding, learning, and actively listening. Be willing to admit when you are wrong, and be open to rewriting the unconscious script you may have created for your partner. Recognise that each moment of interaction is a fresh opportunity for discovery. You can only know your partner to the extent that you know yourself.

Observe yourself and your loved ones to notice how words, body language, spoken messages, and unspoken expressions play a role in your communication styles.

Communication has a rhythm and style. It can be emotional or neutral. Powerful or gentle. Fast-paced or serene. It can be functional, inquisitive, creative, or playful, serving as an invitation to self-discovery and a pathway to exploring the vast internal world of your relational partner.

### Explore this Further

How do you express yourself? Are you playing safely in the shallows—and not showing your true self? Or do you go deep, wading and diving into the waters of your emotions and your needs—daring to risk exposure? Are you willing to go beyond habit and step with grace into the realms of your imagination and reveal who you are to them? And to yourself?

How about your loved ones? How do they express themselves to you? What can you learn about them? What are their intentions, desires and needs, and what do they want you to know? Who are they? Who are you? Stay curious.

To communicate richly with them, you must go deeper within yourself. To begin the process of genuinely understanding yourself in all your magnificent glory—wounds, fears, resistance, habits and all! Are you willing? Are they?

Knowing your particular level of commitment to being known and seen by your partner, and their willingness to be seen, heard and known too, is the litmus test to recognising how deep your connection and intimacy will go together.

If you or they require greater depth, it is time to be radically honest with one another and consciously decide to either go all in or assess whether it is time to move on.

If you require more and are willing to do the work to foster emotional safety and create a relationship that inspires you, healthy and conscious communication is the heart and soul of your relational intimacy and ever-expanding connection with yourself and the other.

This will call for courageousness, trust, and intentional listening—of your inner world, along with you showing up and hearing your partner—with an unwavering commitment to bringing your best self forward, especially when it becomes challenging and you find yourself slipping backwards.

The art of sacred communication is how we wake up to and explore all avenues and expressions of communication, from body language to spoken and unspoken words.

In Practice:

When collaborating with couples, our initial emphasis is on fostering clear and respectful communication rooted in an open and loving heart. Unfortunately, this crucial aspect often goes overlooked in many relationships, leading to unacknowledged and unexpressed needs, resentments, and fears. The cornerstone of emotional intimacy lies in transparent communication, a readiness to be vulnerable and honest, and the ability to both receive and be received without the fear of judgment. Building emotional safety, dismantling barriers, and cultivating a mutual desire to deeply understand one another are fundamental aspects within any relationship.

# YOUR ATTACHMENT STYLE

*Recognising your relational and emotional attachment style will support you in your desire to work towards a more secure attachment style as you foster healthier and more fulfilling relationships.*

If you are to develop emotional intimacy within the container of your relationship, you must understand your and your partner's attachment style. There are many layers to this aspect of the work, but it is worth diving in.

Anxious and avoidant relational dynamics represent two distinct attachment styles that you may exhibit in romantic relationships. These attachment styles are often described as opposites, with each desiring the opposite experience than they habitually demonstrate. Let's look into these dynamics and explore how they manifest in relationships.

## Anxious Attachment

Individuals with an anxious attachment style tend to seek high levels of emotional intimacy and closeness in their relationships. They often worry about their lover's availability and commitment, fearing abandonment or rejection. Some key characteristics of anxious attachment include:

### Desire for Closeness

Anxious individuals crave emotional closeness, reassurance, and frequent communication with their partners. They may feel most secure when they are in constant contact.

### Fear of Abandonment

They have a fear of being left alone or rejected by their partner. This fear can lead to clinginess, jealousy, and attempts to control their partner's actions.

### Intense Emotional Responses

Anxious individuals may experience heightened emotional reactions to relationship issues, such as extreme sadness or anxiety if they perceive their partner to be distant or unavailable.

### Desiring the Opposite Experience

Anxious individuals often choose avoidant partners, as this affords them the time apart and spaciousness that they internally desire, this is the opposite of how their attachment style externally manifests. They may long for a sense of self-sufficiency, independence, and autonomy but struggle without constant reassurance. If you recognise yourself in this style of relating, your personal and relational growth comes from developing security and stability within yourself.

### Avoidant Attachment

Individuals with an avoidant attachment style tend to prioritize independence and self-sufficiency in their relationships. They may feel uncomfortable with too much emotional intimacy and may often seek space and distance from their partners. Key characteristics of avoidant attachment include:

### Desire for Independence

Avoidant individuals value their independence and may feel suffocated or overwhelmed when a partner becomes too emotionally demanding or dependent.

### Difficulty with Vulnerability

They may struggle to express their own emotions or respond to their partner's emotional needs, often downplaying the importance of emotional connection.

### Fear of Enmeshment

Avoidant individuals fear losing themselves in the relationship, which can lead to emotional distancing, reluctance to commit, and a tendency to prioritise self-reliance.

### Desiring the Opposite Experience

Avoidant individuals often desire the opposite of what their attachment style indicates. You may yearn for deeper emotional connection, a greater ability to express vulnerability, and a sense of comfort with emotional intimacy. You may want to experience the security and support that comes from being emotionally available and responsive partners in your relationships. Valuing and leaning into vulnerability and creating emotional intimacy is your key area of personal growth. If you relate to this style of being in a relationship, your personal and relational growth comes from developing intimacy, presence and safety within closeness, both with yourself and with a significant other.

### Navigating Change

Recognising and understanding these attachment styles is the first step towards creating healthier relational dynamics. In these examples, the attachment styles have been simplified to give you a taste of two dominant attachment styles.

Both anxious and avoidant individuals can work towards achieving a more secure attachment style, which involves:

---

## Self-awareness

Understanding your attachment style and its impact on your relationships

## Communication

Explore your needs, fears, and desires with your partner.

## Support

Seek relationship mentoring or counselling to explore and address underlying attachment-related issues.

## Self-development

Work on personal growth and self-esteem to reduce dependence on external validation or excessive independence.

Anxious and avoidant attachment styles often desire experiences contrary to their habitual patterns. As you recognise these internal desires and work towards more secure attachments you can embody and create healthier and more fulfilling relationships.

The given examples are generalisations, you are unique, as is your partner, be curious, remain open and explore your inner world and outer relating patterns to develop your relationship and capacity to be present, secure and unwavering in your connection. There are other iterations of attachment styles that you may wish to explore (reference the recommended reading list at the back of this book to support you further).

# DO YOU FIND YOUR PARTNER FASCINATING?

*Your partner lives in a world entirely of their own, it may well exist side by side with yours, but nonetheless, their own daily and lifelong experiences are beyond your own perceptions as you are consumed with living your own relative reality.*

In the intricate dance of love, you find yourself drawn into the orbit of your beloved. Their presence becomes a constant in your life, a companion on your journey through this intricate world. You share moments, space, and dreams, yet there's an enigma you may overlook—the fact that your partner lives in a world entirely of their own.

It's a world that might exist parallel to yours but is uniquely theirs. Their daily and lifelong experiences, along with the beliefs and the projections that inhabit their mind, are an intricate interplay within their consciousness. And though you stand side by side, hold one another, and make decisions together, their world remains beyond your perceptions. You are absorbed in your relative reality, your inner universe, as they are most concerned with their own.

When was the last time you ventured into this intimate space? When did you most recently pause, look beyond the familiar, and reach out to touch the essence of your partner's being? When did you delve into their experiences? Have you been exploring their beliefs and secret desires to unearth the truth that resides in the heart of their inner world? When did you decide you knew who they were, what they wanted and needed, and forgot to remain curiously open to the possibility that they, like you, are evolving?

Finding your partner fascinating is a journey of curiosity and empathy. It's a decision to not just coexist but to truly connect on a profound level. It's about embracing the mystery that dwells within the one you love, understanding that there are layers upon layers to uncover, like pages in a never-ending story.

Are you captivated by the inner workings of your lover's mind, by the subtle nuances that make them who they are? Are you curious enough to explore the unknown, to venture into uncharted territory with them? If not, why not? Love, after all, is an exploration, a creative journey that requires your loving attention, growth, and sincere devotion to each of you becoming your most magnificent self.

To find your partner fascinating is to be an active and reflective participant in their journey of self-discovery, just as they are in yours. It is to be willing to witness their growth and evolution and to provide unwavering support as they transform into the best version of themselves. It's about being their confidant, cheerleader, and partner. Become the unwavering love you seek by supporting them as they evolve into being more of a wholesome protagonist in the lived expression of their unique story.

So, take a moment to ponder—do you find your partner fascinating? And if you do, cherish that fascination. Embrace it, nurture it, and let it guide you in an exploration of their inner world, for within those depths, you may discover a love more profound and meaningful than you ever imagined.

# PLEASURE AS A STATE OF BEING

*What you are seeking exists within. As you turn your awareness inwards you reveal, and revel in, all you desire.*

In the experience of life, pleasure stands as one of its most exquisite states of being. It is the sensual joy of being alive, fully present, and open to the world of imagination and manifestation around you. More than a fleeting sensation, pleasure can become a profound and spiritual state, a gateway to a deeper connection with the universe and yourself.

Imagine moving through the world where you consciously invite pleasure into your life as an integral part of your existence. You would savour the warming deliciousness of the sun on your skin, the gentle caress of the breeze and the melody of birdsong, and the aroma of blooming flowers. You would revel in the exquisite taste of a perfectly ripe piece of fruit and the sensation of your feet meeting the earth with every step. This becomes a testament to your capacity to embrace the gift of being alive.

Pleasure is more than just a superficial pursuit; it is a profound exploration of the senses, a sacred dance with the tangible and the intangible, and an acknowledgement of the intricate interplay between your physical and spiritual selves. By immersing yourself in pleasure, you open your heart to the beauty and wonder of the world, and you come to understand that your connection with the universe is not merely cerebral but deeply visceral. This is almost an innocent, childlike wonder at the magic and beauty of the world. Imagine how this state of awareness could nourish your life experiences and relationships.

To embrace pleasure as a spiritual state of being is to recognize that it transcends the confines of hedonism. It is not about indulgence but about mindful presence, about becoming attuned to the subtle and profound experiences that make life a true and wondrous journey of meaning. In these moments, you are not just a spectator you are a participant in the wild interplay of existence.

You may access your inner realms through pleasure, where your soul meets the material realms, and you can know yourself beyond your typical socialised expressions. When you connect with the essence of your humanity, without rejection, and with a state of fascinated awareness, coupled with your capacity to love, to experience bliss, and to create. Pleasure ignites your creative spark as you become inspired by the profound beauty and joy around you.

In this state of being playfully aware and pleasurably open, you become magnetic, intoxicating, and deeply attractive. You understand that pleasure is not selfish but rather a gift we give ourselves to replenish our inner reserves and the present we offer others when we share our exuberance and love. It is a way of acknowledging the interconnectedness of all living things, an affirmation that the universe delights in our existence and invites us to reciprocate that delight. As we embrace pleasure as a spiritual state of being, we uncover a profound truth that the universe itself is a source of boundless sensuality alive in each moment of recognition.

When you invite pleasure into your life as a cherished companion on your spiritual journey, you will understand that pleasure is not a distraction from your path. Conversely, it is an integral part of it. Through pleasure, you awaken to your aliveness, becoming more attuned to the beauty of existence and more aware of your connection to all that is sacred and pure.

Imagine creating moments of profound connection with your loved one, where you both feel attuned, in harmony and with pleasure coursing through your experiences together. Is this something you desire? Have you felt the magnetic pull and intoxication of being so liberated within yourself that this nourishes your interactions and relational intimacy with your partner?

As you explore the practices within this book, you open the doorway to experiencing more pleasure in your life.

In the embrace and expression of pleasure, you find spiritual fulfilment and a profound state of being that is your birthright. Savour the world, for in its pleasures you may encounter the divine, and in your heart, you become a vessel for the universe's boundless love.

# CONSCIOUS LOVING AND SPIRITUAL TURN ON

*Sacred sexuality is a divine portal to expanded consciousness and intentional living.*

In a fast-paced world filled with distractions and demands, it is essential to your well-being to create ways to reconnect with your inner self and cultivate more meaningful experiences. One powerful avenue for doing just that is conscious lovemaking. This intimate and spiritual practice not only nourishes your relationships but also enriches your overall well-being, ultimately enhancing the quality of your life.

In the realm of lovemaking exists a profound and enchanting dimension that transcends the physical. It's the world of conscious lovemaking and the spiritual turn-on. This is a sacred dance between two souls. It offers an intimate connection that awakens the spirit and nourishes the heart. This spiritual turn-on goes beyond the mundane, and it's a pathway to transcendent experiences that can enrich your life in ways you never thought possible.

Conscious lovemaking is an intimate practice that requires presence and a genuine connection between partners. It's about elevating the act of physical love into a spiritual journey, where two people come together not just as bodies but as beings with intricate emotions and souls, where a recognition of the eternal essence of one another is appreciatively honoured. In conscious lovemaking, the focus isn't solely on the destination but on the journey itself. It's about cherishing each moment, each touch, every breath, and every sigh.

Spiritual turn-on could be referred to as soulful intimacy. It is the moment when the physical and emotional connections between partners lead to a profound spiritual and energetic experience. It's the feeling of oneness, of being connected to something greater than yourself. To experience Spiritual Seduction affords you a profoundly moving experience and a sanctuary of depth and

---

authenticity. These experiences can enhance your life by nurturing your spiritual eternal selfhood and reminding you of the beauty and spirituality that is alive within you in every intimate moment.

In essence, you move beyond the transient experiences of the physical world. In doing so, you recognise the part of you that is timeless and interconnected with a greater universal reality—and in some interpretations—the ultimately undying essence. It's a concept that speaks to the enduring nature of the self and its connection to something greater than and beyond the individual human experience.

Conscious lovemaking and spiritual turn-on are about more than just physical satisfaction. It is a holistic approach to intimacy that emphasises presence, openness, communication, and mindful presence. In conscious lovemaking, in the arms of your lover, you open yourself to an experience of all that is holy, pure and divine. Perhaps you have had glimmers of this profound and intoxicating state of open reverie? Has your love taken you to church? To God?

Conscious lovemaking can have a significant role to play in enhancing your life as it encourages open-hearted connection beyond your habitual edge of closure. This helps you build trust and strengthens the emotional bonds with your partner. It allows you to let go of worries about the past or future and savour the experience of the present moment.

Incorporating conscious lovemaking into your life takes practice and intention. It involves not just physical connection but emotional and spiritual connection as well. This commitment and investment of time and effort may support you in maintaining a powerful emotional bond outside of the bedroom.

Conscious lovemaking is a beautiful journey of self-discovery, intimacy, and connection that can enhance your life profoundly. By approaching lovemaking with mindful respect and loving intention, you can experience a deeper level of fulfilment and connection that expands beyond the act itself. By practising conscious lovemaking, you can strengthen your closeness with your partner, experience heightened pleasure, and develop your consciousness through the power of sexual intimacy. This may lead you to navigate challenges more effectively and experience greater satisfaction in your relationship. Ultimately, this practice has the potential to transform not only your relationships but also your entire life, leading to a more profound sense of well-being and contentment.

Here are some elements of conscious lovemaking for you to explore as you create a sense of oneness and interconnectedness with your partner and the cosmic universe:

**Presence**

To experience expanded consciousness during intimacy, it is essential to be present in the moment. This means letting go of distracting thoughts so that you may focus your attention on your body, sensations, and your partner. You can practice mindfulness techniques to help you foster a state of presence.

## Open Communication

Communication is vital to conscious lovemaking. This means being open and honest with your partner about your desires, aspirations, and boundaries for your love. It also means actively listening to your partner and responding to their cues. Understanding each other's intentions can foster a deeper spiritual connection.

## Meditation

Practising meditation can help you stay present during lovemaking and foster spiritual awareness.

## Connection

Conscious lovemaking is about creating an energetic connection with your partner. This can involve eye contact, physical touch, playfulness, and emotional intimacy.

## Intention

Setting intentions for your lovemaking can help you stay focused and create a more meaningful experience. This could be as simple as deciding to be present or to focus on sensation.

## Sensuality

Conscious lovemaking is about experiencing pleasure and sensuality in the moment. This could involve exploring different sensations and erogenous zones, using touch, scent, or sound to enhance the experience.

## Embrace Vulnerability

Don't be afraid to express your emotions and vulnerabilities with your partner, it is through these moments of authenticity that deep connections are forged.

## Energetic Sensitivity

Cultivating an awareness of the energy flow within both your and your partner's body, as well as the subtle realms, is crucial for expanding conscious awareness. Engage in energy practices, delve into the exploration of chakras, and incorporate breathwork to enhance your ability to guide energy. This may lead you to heightened connection, vibrant sensuality, and a profound spiritual awakening.

## Create a Sacred Space

Set the mood by creating a sacred environment that encourages intimacy and spiritual connection.

Embrace these elements to cultivate a profound and uplifting love within yourself and your partner. By doing so, you will experience being Spiritually Seduced, deepening your connection to the divine, both individually and in the sacred contours of your shared life.

# EXPLORING DIVINE FEMININE AND DIVINE MASCULINE ENERGIES

*Tapping into the divine masculine and divine feminine energies can enhance intimacy and connection in a relationship and create a more fulfilling sexual experience.*

The concept of divine feminine and masculine energies has deep roots in various spiritual and cultural traditions. These polar opposite energies symbolise fundamental aspects of the universe and are believed to permeate everything, including ourselves. Divine Feminine energy embodies receptivity, intuition, nurturing, compassion, and creativity. It's often visualised as a goddess, the moon, or a mother figure, characterised by care and love—it is the gentle yet powerful, nurturing force that allows you to connect with your emotions, creativity, and the subtle aspects of life and the mysteries held within yourself and the universe. Divine masculine energy is often associated with strength, logic, assertiveness, and action. It's commonly represented as a god, father figure, or the sun and is known for protection and decisiveness—it's the driving force that propels you to set goals, take action, and bring order to chaos.

Together, these energetic signatures and aspects of consciousness make up the two halves of one unified whole. The dance between the two is where the relationship with your beloved occurs. Crucially, these energies are not confined to any specific gender or sex. They exist in all individuals irrespective of their biological sex or gender identity. Both men and women possess both feminine and masculine energies. Striking a balance between these energetics internally creates a wholesome presence and is vital for a healthy and harmonious life.

There has been a resurgence of interest in the divine feminine energy in recent years. It's viewed as a counterbalance to the prevailing patriarchal structures and values in our society, many believe reconnecting with the divine feminine energy may help create a more compassionate, nurturing, and balanced world. Do you agree?

Exploring these energies involves specific practices such as meditation, yoga, dance, energy work or ritual ceremonies that honour the divine feminine and masculine. Delving into the myths and stories of various cultures can also deepen your understanding of masculine and feminine consciousness. Ultimately, the journey of exploring these energetic expressions is personal and ongoing. This requires you to be open to embracing your strengths and vulnerabilities and cultivate balance and harmony within yourself and in your relationships with others. Understanding the feminine and masculine energies within yourself and your partner is essential for nurturing healthy and fulfilling relationships.

To comprehend these energies within yourself, start by recognising your strengths, weaknesses, tendencies, and behaviour patterns. For instance, if you tend to be more nurturing and compassionate, you may express more feminine energy, while assertiveness and goal orientation might indicate a potent masculine energy. There is no right or wrong way to express or experience these energies, and each has unique strengths and challenges. You will find that you tend to operate with a more feminine or masculine flavour but display the opposite qualities in relevant circumstances. The trick is to be able to switch states as required during the moment. For example, if you are a feminine essence woman and work in a male-dominated environment it can become a habit for you to hold the outwardly focused attention of masculine energy, as required by the job, long after you return home. With awareness and specific practices, you may soften this state and radiate your feminine flow for the benefit of yourself, your lover, and your home.

To understand these energies in your partner, observe their behaviour, communication style, and values. Engage in open and honest conversations to understand their unique expression of these energies. Respect and honour each other in your masculine or feminine preference and work together to find a harmonious balance. For instance, if one partner leans towards expressing more feminine energy, the other can balance with more masculine energy and vice versa. You may, with practice, choose to switch these states as an act of love to support your partner in becoming more of their true self.

In the sacred realm of love, a beautiful dance unfolds—a harmonious interplay of divine energies that beckons partners to embark on a journey of both passion and spiritual unity. This intricate dance hinges on equilibrium, as masculine and feminine elements intertwine and complement each other, creating a tapestry of ecstasy beyond physical boundaries. Masculine presence acts as a sturdy foundation, offering stability and security akin to the solid earth beneath one's feet. It establishes a safe and sacred foundation for the dance of love. On the other hand, the feminine aspect contributes emotional depth, intuition, a free-flowing creative spirit, and a spectrum of variety. A robust connection to grounded presence allows the uninhibited expression of feminine vitality, enticing the masculine into a profound connection and reverence for the sacred feminine. Together, these contrasting facets and expressions of consciousness find their unique balance within oneself and in the intricate dance of a relationship.

This dance is not confined to the realms of light. It also embraces the shadows. Love acts as a revealing force, laying bare triggers, fears, and needs, allowing partners to acknowledge and embrace the darker dimensions of consciousness. This interplay of opposites becomes a transformative journey, enriching expressions of love in its brilliance and shadows.

These shadows, when illuminated, add depth and intensity to the dance, turning it into a journey of self-discovery and mutual growth if embraced with a willing heart and integrity. Exploring the interplay of these forces—the yin and yang, the light and dark, the push and pull reveals true ecstasy and spiritual fulfilment. As you delve into your relationship, you learn to navigate desire, intimacy, and vulnerability, weaving them into a tapestry of divine connection. In this dance, positions or states of consciousness transition seamlessly when both partners remain open-hearted and authentically attentive—a dynamic exchange with moments of leadership and followership, each partner learning from and understanding the other—a dance of discovery, a play of intimacy and attuned understanding of the other, where both partners are powerful in their unique expressions.

## Your Masculine Challenge

As a masculine force, your challenge lies in leading with an open heart for the Highest Good, not for immediate satisfaction or to please your partner. True and lasting respect comes from committing to your purpose daily, eliminating guesswork, and displaying a strongly aligned inner direction. Your problem-solving abilities make you attractive to your feminine partner, allowing her to relax and express her essence. Being fully present without distraction or judgment fosters a deep connection between you and your partner. Mastering this earns her loving respect. Clear boundaries enable profound openness, and the ability to shift into empathetic responsiveness is crucial for a harmonious connection. Your challenge is to be discerning and wise and choose a life partner to commit to. This will enhance your life as she shares her heart with you.

## Your Feminine Challenge

Your challenge as a feminine-identified being is to let down your guard and allow yourself to soften, flow with your intuition, and NOT direct or fix your partner. You are invited to find ways to relax into your sensual and earthy nature to nourish yourself and your loved ones. This will feel so juicy and alive for you. If you work in a more masculine environment, you must let go of the striving and need to get things done before or as soon as you get home so that you may be in your natural receptive state of receivership—an inwards-focused state of being. If you are high-achieving in your work, your heart and your partner's heart require you to let go and be in your feminine essence for most of the time you are together. Your masculine essence partner finds this alluring. Your lover wants to feel your body and emotions as aliveness. He wants to provide for you and have your heart trust and respect him. You are challenged to find a partner with whom you can fully express yourself and rest in his leadership without losing yourself or needing to change him to please you.

# HOW TO HONOUR AND BALANCE MASCULINE AND FEMININE ENERGIES

*Where two souls entwine, there exists a dance of divine energies waiting to be explored.*

**Masculine:** Outward focused, attention on problem–solving, observing, directing, and leading.
**Feminine:** Internal awareness, the attention placed upon, receptive, creative, and being seen.

As you embark on this journey of balancing and honouring your masculine and feminine energies, remember that it's not a destination but a lifelong exploration. The energetic dance within you and your relationship is as unique as your fingerprint and becomes a journey of self-discovery and self-acceptance that unfolds with time.

This is non-gender specific, but rather, a dance and interplay of polarised opposites, with each person embodying the consciousness of outward or inward-focused attention to greater and lesser degrees. Exploring these energies can lead to a lifetime of learning, integration, and discovery. When exhibiting masculine consciousness, you will be focused on finding solutions as you get things done. Your attention is outside yourself upon people, places, and things. When alive with feminine consciousness, you will be in a feeling state of creative expression, playfulness and rest. You will have the attention upon you, causing you to turn inward. In your intimate relationship, during conversation and play, one will lead whilst the other receives—play with this—backwards and forwards as a dance of exquisite nourishment to see and to be seen. To lead and be led. To direct and be directed.

Honouring and balancing masculine and feminine energies as a sacred dance in a relationship can create a profound and harmonious connection and a beautiful interplay of sensual aliveness, nourishment, and direction for the flow of love to expand. It's a dance that celebrates the richness of life, the depth of emotions, and the power of action. It's a journey towards a more fulfilling, balanced, and interconnected existence. This requires conscious effort from both partners. It is not about pitted against each other. It's about allowing a dance of harmony. Here are some steps to help you find that balance:

## Self-awareness

The first step to balancing the energies is understanding your natural inclinations towards masculine and feminine energies. Learn to recognise your strengths and the areas where you need more balance and personal development.

## Acceptance

Embrace and accept these energies within yourself. Acknowledge that both are equally valuable and essential for personal growth and well-being.

## Communication

Communication is a fundamental aspect of any relationship. Please encourage others to express their feelings and thoughts freely, creating a safe space for emotional connection.

## Mutual respect

You and your partner should respect each other's dominant energy expression and not try to change or suppress it. Instead, you could appreciate and honour each other's unique strengths.

## Let Go of Stereotypes

Release societal stereotypes and expectations about how masculinity and femininity should manifest in your life. Embrace what feels authentic to you.

## Creative Expression

Explore your creativity, whether it be through art, music, or any form of self-expression. This is a beautiful way to awaken your sensual energy.

## Self-Care

Please prioritise self-care to nurture your emotional well-being. This can include meditation, yoga, time in nature, or engaging in activities that soothe and enliven your soul.

## Shared responsibilities

Both partners opt to share responsibilities and work to find balance in all areas of their lives, such as household chores, financial decisions, and parenting, in a manner that allows them to relate from their innate state of consciousness.

## Embrace polarity

Polarity refers to the energy differences between partners that create a frisson of attraction and passion. Both partners are encouraged to embrace and celebrate their differences and amplify them to create a deeper and more fulfilling connection.

## Seek support

If needed, seek support from a therapist, counsellor, or coach who can help you both navigate challenges to balancing your energies and creating a more harmonious relationship.

# YOUR FEMININE DESIRE

*When one woman claims her birthright of sensual aliveness, radiance, magnetism, and power naturally others are inspired to do the same as the whole world is illuminated by her presence.*

The essence of Feminine Consciousness resides in the gentle embrace of love and intimacy. She exudes a playful abundance, blossoming to her fullest potential when she feels open and safe, allowing her inner radiance to flourish. Feminine consciousness resides not only in the love and light girlishness of the unawakened woman—she also lives as the embodiment of the magnetic dark feminine—wildly alive, sensual, evocative and alluring. To fully embrace becoming an awakened feminine being is to embrace all aspects and qualities of the feminine—especially those qualities you may shy away from expressing.

Deep within, you yearn to experience life as a manifestation of love, fully awakened and expressed through your heart, inner strength, sensuality, and wild allure. This longing is essential to crafting a life that resonates with your heart's desires. There exists within the womb of your heart a profound desire to live authentically, unearth the depths of your feminine power and embrace life as an unfiltered expression of your true self as you are seen and felt from the core of your being. Listen to the wise inner voice that sings whispers of inner truth that guide you toward your ultimate expression.

You aspire to flourish and revel in the vibrancy of existence, form supportive connections, appreciate beauty, nurture wellness, and feel erotically alive all while you feel at ease, open, and passionately engaged with the fullness of life. You know that you inherently deserve to reveal the essence of your being, vibrantly alive and thriving in every aspect of your life—even though you often shy away from this truth for fear of being considered a woman who takes up too much space. You yearn for a safe emotional haven where you can bear your heart and emotions without fear of judgment. Your deepest desires are devotion and the fullness of love coursing through your being.

The more you are seen, the more your heart radiates, and the barriers around it melt away. You yearn to move gracefully within your own body, free from any constraints of societal conditioning and unprocessed emotional blocks. Your heart longs for and requires the companionship of other women who share your journey. You desire appreciation, security, care, and the knowledge that you are a top priority in your partner's life.

When emitting a frequency of feminine energy, you are instinctively nurturing and loving towards others. You embrace all of your emotions. You delight in the receiving of others' gifts, energy, time and commitment. You live a life of devotion in reverence to the beauty inherent within each moment, caress, smile, and task. You live as trust and therefore relinquish the need to control. You live with an open heart and an intuitive connection to All That Is whilst expressing your heart's yearnings with reverential respect and a desire to be known. In this manner, you take radical responsibility for how you show up, entering the flow of grace by dancing off any stuck energy and clearing all that holds you back from shining with love.

As the embodiment of feminine consciousness, your inner longing is profound. You seek to connect deeply with your sensual nature and feel safe knowing that your emotions are valid and deserve expression. You deeply yearn to have your needs met as you invite more love into your life and to be seen, heard, voiced and known. You desire a lover who will ravish you beyond the borders of your body and mind into the erotic space of devotional reverence and wild abandon.

The world needs more women who are illuminated, inspired, fully alive, and driven by the profound wisdom of the heart. This is not a luxury but a fundamental necessity. When one woman claims her birthright of sensuous vitality, radiance, and magnetic power, she becomes a beacon that inspires others to follow suit. This creates an inner strength that offers the potential to heal our ancestral lineage and cause a ripple effect of healing across the globe.

Your awakening, vibrant, unfettered heart is required as you realise your potential.

As feminine consciousness collectively rises and awakens HER power, sensuality, and vitality, the world flourishes in response to this potent feminine magic. This becomes the foundation for co-creating a world where we may all thrive, a world built on the pillars of love.

# YOUR MASCULINE DESIRE

*Respect yourself and the whole world opens to you.*

As the demonstration of conscious masculinity, your deepest desire is to transcend the superficial and forge a life anchored in your core values. What you yearn for is not just fleeting surface level connections. As a conscious and mature masculine being, you seek profound and meaningful relationships where you are valued and respected so that your soul feels genuinely fulfilled.

Your aspiration is profound—an authentic relationship where judgment and rejection have no place, a sanctuary where you can wholeheartedly be yourself. In this realm of conscious masculinity, you hold honesty and vulnerability in high regard. They are tools for unburdening your heart and freely sharing your feelings, thoughts, and emotions with your partner. You acknowledge that this can be a challenge, but your heart aches for the embrace of a lover who welcomes your raw authenticity, your potent power, and the surge of passion that lives deep within you.

Beyond the allure of physical attraction, your soul craves emotional intimacy, a space where you can unveil your innermost thoughts, fears, and dreams within the safety of a nurturing cocoon. This fosters a profound connection with your partner and builds trust beyond the superficial. This, in turn, supports your mission and enhances your life beyond measure.

In your journey of conscious masculinity, you are driven by a desire to pursue your passions and purpose to manifest your life's mission and leave a legacy of depth and meaning. You require a partner who supports you and actively encourages your purpose—this is indispensable to you. This partner becomes the recipient of your devoted love and mutual respect. You yearn for a partner who embodies the qualities of devotion, love, receptivity, kindness, and passion. In the sacred dance of individual freedom and interdependence, you place immense value on the strength of a supportive union. Your masculine essence deeply longs for genuine connection and companionship. You cherish relationships where you can be fully present, sharing experiences, laughter, and challenges with your beloved. You seek partners who uphold the values of trust and loyalty and are committed to the partnership with unwavering resolve.

As you embrace your evolving conscious masculinity, you recognise the importance of approaching physical intimacy with care, consent, and emotional connection. You are becoming more attuned to your privilege and seek ways to clear any unresolved blind spots to how you show up as the masculine in the world. You are actively transcending the objectification of the feminine and are committed to exploring and shedding any toxic masculine traits inherited from the collective consciousness.

You desire a relationship where meaningful contributions flow freely between you and your partner. Conscious masculinity is about being in a partnership where both individuals uplift and support one another, working together toward shared goals and values with open hearts and a spirit of playful self-discovery.

You value a feminine-essenced partner who willingly lets down her guard and softens into the grace of her femininity - this nourishes you deep to your core. This woman inspires your heart, activates your protection and provision, and is the lover who initiates you beyond your past closures into bringing your legacy to earth as she unwaveringly supports your mission.

By embracing these desires and fostering a robust masculine consciousness, you nurture relationships imbued with emotional depth, fulfilment, and mutual respect. This journey leads to a well-lived life, profound purpose, and passionately inspired love—an offering to the world, your partner, and your legacy.

In practice:

During a session my masculine-identifying client once told me that he didn't really understand how it felt to be with a deeply feminine woman, his partnerships had been fairly neutral with little sexual polarity. His relationship had become like being housemates, rather than lovers. I taught him an embodied understanding of masculine and feminine states of being. This gave him a chance to track his response and feel how his state switched from one polarity to the other so that he could choose, at any given moment, how he wanted to show up for himself and his partner.

# HAVE YOU FOUND GOD IN THE ARMS OF YOUR LOVER?

*Enter the heart, and love will meet you there.*

Love, they say, is the most sacred of human experiences. It is the force that binds us together, the elixir that fuels our existence. Yet, beneath the surface of passion and desire, there lies a profound truth—a truth that transcends the mundane and the ephemeral. It is the truth of a spiritual connection that awakens within us when we share our most intimate moments with our beloved.

As bodies entwine and souls merge, there is a feeling—a sensation—that cannot be put into words. Have you felt it? It is a feeling of oneness of unity and of being part of something greater than yourself. In those stolen moments of ecstasy and energetic communion, you catch a glimpse of the divine and find yourself drawn into a realm where love and spirituality converge.

It is a time when secrets are whispered between souls, when hearts beat in synchrony, and when the boundary between the physical and the spiritual blurs into obscurity. It is in these moments that you find yourself bathed in the most profound energy of all—you find God in the arms of your lover.

How does being in the arms of your lover bring you closer to God? Is it the touch of their skin, the warmth of their breath, or the intensity of their gaze? Perhaps it is all these things and more—for in love, you are stripped of pretence and ego, and you stand before each other as vulnerable and as human as you could ever be. It is in this vulnerability that you find a connection that transcends the physical—an intimacy that touches the very essence of your being.

Some may argue that God resides in the grandeur of nature, within the silence of a chapel, or in the pages of sacred texts. And indeed, this is true. But the omnipresence of God also resides in the embrace of a lover, in the shared laughter of two souls, and in the tears shed in moments of profound intimacy and earth-shattering ecstasy. The divine is not confined to temples or churches, spiritual bliss is everywhere, and it is in you. This is Spiritual Seduction.

To find God in the arms of your lover is to recognise the divinity within yourself and your partner. It is to see beyond the surface and dive deep into the ocean of love that flows between you. It is to understand that the physical and the spiritual are not separate but intertwined and that the highest form of worship is loving and being loved.

The dance of love is a sacred act of reverence for the part of you that is eternally connected to all that is sacred, holy, and pure. Within the arms of your lover, you find yourself unified beyond all reasoning in cosmic fields of divine beingness and profound love.

It is as if the universe itself conspires to bring you together, to guide your souls on this sacred journey to traverse the winding path of life, face your fears, shed your masks and stand before each other in naked vulnerability. In surrendering to the currents of love, you allow them to sweep you away to uncharted territories of the heart.

In these moments, you are not two bodies entangled in desire but two vessels of the sacred. Your love is a pathway to God, a communion of souls. Love is a prayer and an answer. It is a worshipping of the divine within each other. With this unified awareness and your hearts open to each another, you expand beyond the here and now into pure ecstasy within the quantum realms.

Within the embrace of your lover, take a moment to reflect. Look into their eyes and see the reflection of your soul. Feel the beating of their heart and know that it beats in rhythm with yours. And in that moment, ask yourself: Have I found God in the arms of my lover? The answer—if you dare to seek it, may reveal the most profound truth of all—that love is not just a human experience— it is a divine one.

Terminology:

God: Please insert any word that you would use to describe that which is omniscient, omnipotent, omnipresent. The All That Is, The Divine, The Universe, Cosmic Love, Spirit.
Masculine/Him: The qualities of masculine energy. Not gender specific.
Feminine/Her: The qualities of feminine energy. Not gender specific.

# ILLUMINATE THE WAY TO TRUE CONNECTION

*In the shadows of our souls lie the unpolished facets of our potential for love.*

In the complexity of human consciousness, there exists an aspect of your unconscious self that remains largely hidden from your daily awareness—an aspect known as the shadow. This facet of your inner world, often overlooked and unexplored, plays a pivotal role in your ability to form and sustain conscious, fulfilling relationships. Delving into shadow work is an important pathway toward finding your hidden agendas, limitations, and misunderstandings. These, when you do the work, lead you upon the path of wisdom as you unearth gems of self-awareness and greater understanding about the patterns you bring with you to the shores of your relationship.

## The Formation of the Shadow Self

The shadow self, a term popularised by the Swiss psychiatrist Carl Jung, is a repository of repressed or unacknowledged aspects of our personality. It's a composite of our deepest fears, suppressed desires, unresolved emotional wounds, and unexpressed aspects of our identity. These elements form in response to life experiences, especially during childhood or highly emotive states, when we begin to adapt to societal expectations and familial conditioning. Imagine the young child who's scolded for expressing anger or sadness, or the teenager shamed for not fitting in. Over time, these parts of ourselves are pushed into the shadows, hidden away from our conscious awareness. As we grow, our shadow self accumulates more of these disowned elements, and they can accumulate as unresolved conflicts and emotions. Typically we will find ourselves recreating circumstances in our lives and relationships that mimic this internal psychological split, as our innermost self seeks resolution, so that we may integrate the cast off aspects of self and return to an awareness of wholeness. Do you recognise experiences or areas of your life that seem to come around over and again? This may indicate your shadow self and show you a direct way to wholeness by responding in a new and different manner to the trigger or pattern.

## The Light and Dark Aspects of the Shadow

Within the shadow self, there are both light and dark aspects. The dark aspects are often associated with traits and emotions we consider negative, such as jealousy, anger, and insecurity. These aspects can manifest destructively in our relationships if left unexamined. On the other hand, the light aspects of the shadow hold untapped potential and positive qualities, which, when integrated, can enhance our self-awareness and enrich our relationships.

For instance, embracing our anger and learning to express it healthily might lead to assertiveness, setting healthy boundaries, and standing up for ourselves, ultimately contributing to better communication and understanding in our relationships. Recognising our hidden talents, passions, and creativity can also infuse our connections with vitality and depth.

## Integrating the Shadow for Wholeness

The path to embracing the shadow and nurturing conscious relationships involves a process of integration. It's a journey toward self-discovery and self-acceptance, a process that invites us to confront our hidden fears and desires with courage and compassion. Here are some steps to guide this transformative journey:

## Self-Reflection

Begin by examining your past and current relationships. What patterns do you notice? What emotions and behaviours arise in conflict or moments of vulnerability?

## Self-Acceptance

Acknowledge your shadow without judgment. Accept that these aspects are a part of you, just as much as your conscious self. This step is fundamental in reducing inner resistance.

## Self-Inquiry

Engage in deep self-inquiry. Ask yourself why these shadow aspects exist. What early experiences or conditioning led to their formation?

## Mindful Awareness

Cultivate mindful awareness to identify when your shadow is influencing your thoughts, feelings, and behaviours in each moment. This awareness empowers you to make conscious choices.

## Integration

Gradually integrate the light aspects of your shadow to enhance your strengths and talents. Simultaneously, address the dark aspects with therapeutic techniques, self-compassion, and support from trusted individuals.

## Seeking Support

Consider working with a therapist, relationship coach, or mentor who specialises in shadow work to guide you through the process.

Embracing your shadow and integrating it as a transformative and ongoing journey, one that can profoundly impact your ability to form and sustain conscious, fulfilling relationships. By accepting and nurturing all facets of yourself, you re-remember your innate wholeness and authenticity, thereby allowing for deeper connections and a richer experience of love and companionship in your life.

If we look at the shadow of perfectionism, we see that this manifests as the relentless pursuit of flawlessness and the fear of making mistakes or falling short of exacting high standards. In contrast, acceptance or embracing imperfection involves recognising that it's okay not to be perfect and that it's natural to have flaws and make mistakes in our humanness. It's about being comfortable with one's imperfections and understanding that they don't define one's worth. This shift towards acceptance can lead to reduced stress, increased self-compassion, and a more balanced and healthy approach to life.

### Embracing the Shadow: The Key to Conscious Relationship
Below are ten common shadow qualities you may be experiencing in your relationships, along with their corresponding opposite light quality. Journal to explore each one, explore how you express it and where it originates. There are no rights or wrongs. You are bringing awareness to your unconscious habits to integrate these qualities so that you rest in wholeness.

### 1. Fear/Courage
Embrace your fears and courageously step towards vulnerability in your relationships.
### 2. Self-Doubt/Self-Confidence
Cultivate self-assurance and believe in your worthiness of love and happiness.
### 3. Control/Surrender
Let go of the need to control every aspect of your relationships and allow things to unfold naturally.
### 4. Insecurity/Self-Assuredness
Develop a deep sense of self-assuredness and recognise your value beyond external validation.
### 5. Perfectionism/Self-Acceptance
Embrace your imperfections and learn to accept yourself as you are. This allows others to do the same.
### 6. Neediness/Self-Sufficiency
Develop self-sufficiency and cultivate a sense of inner completeness.
### 7. Avoidance/Engagement
Face your fears, insecurities, and the parts of you you might typically avoid. Explore issues in your relationship with open communication and a willingness to address uncomfortable topics.
### 8. Dependency/Independence
Foster healthy interdependence. This allows each person to thrive individually within the relationship.
### 9. Jealousy/Trust
Build trust in yourself, your partner, and the relationship. Trust that you are worthy of love and respect. Commit to showing up for your promises and commitments.
### 10. Projection/Self-Reflection
Engage in self-reflection to recognise when you are projecting your issues onto your partner. Take radical self-responsibility for your experiences.

Let go of the need to control every aspect of your relationship and allow things to unfold with ease. Working with these shadow qualities and embracing their corresponding light qualities may steer you toward healthier, more fulfilling relationships. Remember that this process may take time. Be patient as you compassionately integrate these aspects of your psyche.

---

## A straightforward exercise for shadow work:

Our tendency is to criticise or idealise in others what we have suppressed or hidden within ourselves, these suppressed qualities reside in the shadows. This encompasses both positive and negative qualities. For instance, phrases like 'They are self-centred,' 'They lack responsibility,' 'They are wealthy and therefore a bad person,' 'He/she is unkind,' and 'He/she is selfish' 'She is too sensitive,' are often projections of our unexamined self onto others. We notice these traits in others because they are reflections of aspects hidden and alive within ourselves.

### 1. Create a list

Write a list of your objections and judgments you have about others. Those traits which annoy and upset you, and have you triggered. Include the qualities you see in others that you don't feel that you could ever become. This brings to light and provides insights into aspects of yourself that need acknowledgement and integration. Additional examples:

- "They're always seeking attention."
- "They're too passive and never take initiative."
- "They're too aggressive and domineering."
- "They're too emotional and irrational."
- "They're too reserved and closed-off."
- "They're too materialistic and shallow."
- "They're too idealistic and disconnected from reality."

### 2. Integration

Once you have your list, acknowledge when you have behaved in the same manner. Reflect on one to three occasions for each statement with honesty and self-compassion. Embracing your full human expression is crucial for moving forward.

### 3. Sit in meditation

Give yourself a few minutes in contemplation and bring to mind, in images or words, how this aspect of you looks and feels like. Feel and locate it in your body. Allow yourself to embrace and accept this part of you, inviting your Higher Self for support. This diminishes their power, allowing a new perspective on yourself and others.

### 4. A return to wholeness

The final stage is to write a paragraph recognising the positive aspects of embodying these qualities. Explore the gifts they bring and how they pave the way for a new, integrated self. Consider how you'll respond from this integrated state.

As you encounter unintegrated aspects reflected in others, especially within intimate relationships, repeat this process. Eventually, your partner's actions may change, or you'll find reduced triggers as these qualities find a comfortable place within your heart. The beauty lies in the transformation of both yourself and your relationships.

## In Practice:

Many years ago, when I started to study metaphysics, I was taught the power of Shadow Work. When I wrote my list of traits in others that got to me, the judgments I harboured and refused to acknowledge. I found it difficult to own the top shadow quality mirrored to me through others. It was 'They are irresponsible parents.' this was a huge revelation for me, having to sit with myself and own that I, too, could be irresponsible as a parent. In owning the truth of it, recognising specific events and incidents when I had been irresponsible as a parent was hugely liberating. It opened within me a space to acknowledge my fallibility, bring the light of this awareness, and apologise to my children for the times I could have done better if I had had the wherewithal to do so.

Another shadow quality I have struggled with throughout my life is perfectionism. I refer to myself now as a recovering perfectionist. In embracing my imperfections, allowing myself to make mistakes, and knowing when my oftentimes impossibly high standards are preventing me from being fully in the moment, I have revealed a greater capacity to sit with the perfectly imperfect human condition in myself and others. I have also learned when it is appropriate to channel this capacity to home in on the details and create immense beauty.

I had a client who was feeling like she couldn't quite move forward and create the life she desired. She looked at her sister, who seemed to have it all, with a little exploration my client said 'It's ok for her because she's beautiful and smart.' We worked with this statement to reveal her projection onto her sister and her justification for why she thought she wasn't good enough, smart enough, or beautiful enough to create what she wanted to in her life. Once my client recognised that she couldn't see in her sister, or in another, what isn't housed within herself she was able to own her dreams and move towards an embodiment of her own innate beauty and smartness.

# YOUR DESIRE: SPEAK THE UNSPEAKABLE

*You cannot decide what you deeply desire—it erupts through you, entices you, and pulls at your heartstrings.*

Desire comes through you. You never choose your desires. They are a part of your soul's expression awaiting your permission. Wanting to be backed by you, to be energised into lived experiences. Your desire is your truth. It is not chosen. You do have the power of choice over whether you access your desire. Hear it. Welcome it. Choose it. You will pull yourself in directions in your life, relationships and work that are not your truth, causing you and others great suffering if your desires go unmet.

Are you willing to acknowledge what experiences you yearn for? Are you bold enough to explore your desires, therefore, your destiny? Are you willing to keep shoving your secret desires down—swallowing them along with all your unmet needs to fit in, be acceptable, and not rock the boat? Are you so determined to be detached from your desire—your truth—to the repression of your genius—a gift to all?

You cannot decide what you deeply desire—it erupts through you, entices you, and pulls at your heartstrings. With constant questing and instant presence, it urges you to say yes. You are required to shout yes. YES to love. YES to life. YES to yourself. You know what you want. Will you boldly heed the ancient siren call? Will you trust in your truth—in your desires—to lead you upon the rightful path of your becoming? Especially when you see no evidence that anyone else has done so before?

Will you breathe life and love into your experiences by showing up embodied as your desires? Not shying away or intellectualising them. They cannot be intellectualised. They are not from the mind. But sacred callings from the depth of your soul. Divine callings. Sacred asks. God's Will and your divine path.

Your desires will have you. They will come upon you when you least expect it. They will grab you by the balls and settle uncomfortably within the womb of your longings. They will demand to be respected.

Your unspeakable desires—those dreams you've been hiding from, pushing away and dismissing, want you. And you want them. They're not going anywhere. And neither are you—until you wake up and allow your desires to light your way forward to the life you yearn for.

When not living your dreams and not being fully surrendered to your desires, you will have much to complain about and have many experiences of low-grade disillusionment. What is it that you complain about? What hurts your tender heart and has you feeling unseen and unmet? Your complaints hide a desire. Go digging. Explore. Excavate the truth and desires from beneath the surface-level complaints. Set yourself free.

Your desires will pull you out of the comfortable, slow death you are entertaining right here where you are—dying at the hands of the life you sensibly chose—rather than risking the one that makes you feel alive.

Your sacred desires demand that you create the relationship you dream of and urge you on towards your sexual awakening. And those dreams that demand you put down the tired job or retire that business you've long outgrown, whilst the deep desire to become a parent—even though the timing seems off, begs your acknowledgement and activation. Your needs will have you.

The desires that would have you travelling the world and moving beyond the borders and familiar shores of your current thinking and pent-up frustrations and the desires that know you have more inside of you and are desperate to be acknowledged whilst suffocating under your own internalised repression.

What do you desire?.Do you utter it into the pillow at night? Do you share your truth with your beloved? Do you speak the unspeakable and feel heard and encouraged to become who you were born to be? Are you creating the relational dynamics where you and your lover can be fully seen, accepted and mutually empowered to live your desires upon the rightful path of your destiny?

# CREATING CONNECTION:
# ENHANCING ATTRACTION

*Prioritise each other to reignite the spark of attraction and ask yourself:
What would love have me be and do?*

When you first engaged in a relationship with your loved one, there was no question of your connection and attraction to one another. It was simply a fact, although perhaps over time, you both took it for granted. This attraction existed as the backdrop to building your relationship together. Without the desire to know the other, or indeed yourself, through their eyes, there would be no reason to engage in developing a relationship beyond the first spark of curiosity.

Do you remember the feeling of attraction, desire, and ease you felt with your partner? You may still be experiencing these same fluttering sensations many years along the timeline of your partnership and ready to go deeper. If you close your eyes and turn within, you will be able to tap into this sensation of attraction and desire for your lover in your body. You will notice that it is still simmering, ready to be rekindled with loving passion, curiosity and creative exploration.

The embers of love ignite into the kind of fire that is sustainable when nurtured and fed in a way that creates polarity within your unified wholeness, emotional safety, and a commitment to rising and growing in love. You know that you are called to this sacred path of spiritual seduction with yourself and your loved one.

In this book, you will learn practices to recognise the gifts your lover has within to bestow upon the sacred ground of your union whilst you reveal yours too. When you release the fear of being seen, heard and met by liberating yourself beyond the habits of the past to create an appreciation of the present moment in its ever-changing form.

As the Masculine Consciousness in your relationship, your purpose, passion, mission, direction, and discernment are required to enable yourself to be held to your deepest desires and highest calling. Your intimate relationship is transformed by your clear relational commitment and open-hearted leadership, which creates a safe container for love to deepen and flourish.

When your feminine lover feels safe, relaxed, and held, she will be fully committed to serving the relationship with her loving radiance, and the variety she can play through her body will be behind you in living your mission. She will nourish you in ways you never imagined when she feels the full force of your devotional commitment.

As the feminine consciousness in your relationship, you are gifted with the unique expression of love and playfulness to nourish and ignite your masculine lovers' presence. This is a sacred gift for yourself and your partner. By being playful, clearly and emotively expressed, and relaxed in your body, you invite your partner to let down his stress and reveal his heart.

As you dedicate yourself and your relationship to evolving beyond its current paradigm and story of relating, the practices will support you in deepening your connection with one another as you prioritise each other and reignite the spark of attraction.

When you explore the practices later in this book, you may begin with practice number one and work through them sequentially, or you can choose as you feel called to.

# CO-CREATE YOUR RELATIONSHIP ON YOUR TERMS.

*As you commit yourself to the growth and development of your relationship, the practices within this book will aid you in nurturing emotional freedom and enhancing intimacy, all the while strengthening your bond and helping you both become the best versions of yourselves.*

When you first met your lover, you found time to play, connect, and relax with each other. But as you became more familiar with each other and less intoxicated by discovering the inner world of your beloved, other commitments began to creep in, and you perhaps found yourself missing the closeness and bonding you once shared. If you have managed to maintain a sense of dating one another despite the ever-increasing demands upon your time, then adding the practices in this book to your together time will open up a greater capacity to truly see and experience one another with joy, vulnerability, and playfulness, as you both develop a greater capacity to hold one another and build trust in the container of your union.

You may feel vulnerable when exploring these practices. Please be compassionate and respectful with one another as you develop the energetic capacity to be more fully present, open, and steady within yourself and each other. Prioritise each other and reignite the spark of attraction, closeness, and love from within. In doing so, you create a safe space to explore your individual and relational inner worlds.

After each sacred practice time together, share your experience with your lover. As your partner shares, please avoid jumping in and commenting. Let them express what they need to and receive them with open curiosity. You may close the space with a hug, gratitude, and appreciation for your significant other. If anything complicated comes up, journal about it, please get support and don't bring it up during conflict. You are developing a safe and sacred space to be vulnerable, open, and intimate within yourself so that you may consciously co-create your relational dynamics with heart and soul. A newly emergent paradigm of relationships exists beyond your current relational thinking, actions, and beliefs.

# The Practices

These rituals transcend the boundaries of the mundane. They delve into the mystical realm of emotional and energetic intimacy, where your explorations in love are woven with threads of presence and connection. These practices have been curated for you and your beloved, guiding you towards a harmonious and enriching union that honours the essence of your unique relationship, so you both feel cherished and celebrated, creating a sacred space where deep connection and profound intimacy shall flourish. Use this book as a guide, implementing the practices that resonate most with you.

# SETTING THE SCENE

## OPENING RITUAL

To create the relationship you've been yearning for you will find that commitment to your relational vision is a key step towards shedding old patterns and habits in how you connect, communicate and react. Make it a goal to engage with these practices at least once a week.

Setting the stage and establishing your intention is crucial in creating a safe and welcoming space for both of you. Regardless of your relational status, your relationship is a unique and sacred contract with its own distinctive essence.

By dedicating time to consciously attune to the energy and purpose of your relationship you will be better equipped to navigate the changes that naturally come as you evolve together. The effects of this intentional practice extend far beyond your time together, creating a ripple of positive transformation.

**Creating an Intentional Container for Your Practice:**

**Choose a regular time and space for your weekly practice.**
Select a cosy spot, whether it's your bedroom, a snug den, or the living room, but ensure it's a private and distraction-free area. Arrange for childcare, tie up loose ends, and complete your to-do lists in advance to fully immerse yourself without interruptions.

**Create the ambience.**
Enhance the atmosphere by playing beautiful music, lighting candles, having soft blankets and cushions within reach, diffusing essential oils, and wearing comfortable clothing that makes you feel at ease.

**Determine the practice and its duration.**
In advance, decide which practice you both intend to explore. Ensure you have this book, a journal, pens, blankets, and tissues readily available. Turn off all potential distractions, placing your phones and laptops outside the room.

**Enter the space with a gentle, open, and curious mindset.**
Step into the designated space with the intention to be open, vulnerable, and inquisitive. Be fully present and attentive to both your own and your partner's experiences.

**Communicate with love, without judgment.**
During the practice, engage in open, loving communication without casting judgment on your partner. Remember, there is no 'right' or 'wrong' here. Keep the discussions within this sacred space and refrain from bringing them up during conflicts outside of your practice sessions.

**Be clear about your intentions and the intimacy you create together.**
Articulate your intentions clearly, and acknowledge the intimate space you're co-creating with your partner.

**After your practice time, gently close the space.**
Following your practice, gracefully conclude your session, maintaining the sanctity of the space you've built.

Top Tip:

Decide, ahead of time, which one of you will be setting up the space before your practice session together.

This is a fundamental part of the practice that fosters intentionality and reverence for creating a safe, loving, and supportive space for you to be contained within your love for one another.

# CLOSING RITUAL

## A NEW PARADIGM OF RELATIONSHIP

Closing rituals are a beautiful way for you to conclude your intimacy practice sessions. These rituals can help create a sense of closure and connection, allowing both partners to reflect on their progress and maintain the positive energy generated during the session. Here's a suggested closing ritual:

### The Closing Ritual

### Hand in Hand

Sit or stand facing each other, and take each other's hands. Hold them gently, and take a moment to make eye contact.

### Gratitude

Begin by expressing your gratitude for your partner's presence and willingness to engage in the practices. You can say something like, "I am grateful for the time we've spent together and for your commitment to our relationship."

### Reflect

Take a moment to reflect on the insights and experiences you've had during the practices. Share what you've learned and how it has impacted your relationship.

### Affirmation

Each partner can take turns affirming the positive qualities and efforts of their significant other. Say something you appreciate or admire about your partner. For example, "I appreciate your kindness and patience in our journey together."

### Shared Intentions

Discuss your intentions moving forward. What do you both want to continue working on or improving in your relationship? Share your desires and aspirations.

## Closing Statement

Together, create a closing statement that encapsulates your commitment to one another. For example, "We are committed to growing and deepening our connection. We will continue to nurture our love and support each other."

## Sealing the Ritual

To seal the ritual, you can share a gentle kiss, a hug, or simply hold each other for a few moments in silence. Feel the energy and connection between you both.

## Symbolic Action

As a symbolic gesture, you might extinguish the candles together, signifying the end of the session and the transition back to everyday life.

## Gratitude Again

Finally, express your gratitude once more for the time you've shared during the session. Say something like, "Thank you for being a part of this journey with me."

This closing ritual can help you feel more connected, valued, and focused on your shared goals. It's an opportunity to celebrate your progress and reinforce your commitment to one another.

Top Tip:

Decide ahead of time which one of you will be tidying up the practice space after your practice session together.

This is a fundamental part of the practice that allows you to close the space lovingly before consciously moving on to the next activity or phase of the day.

# 01

## Breathe Together
### Loving Connection and Relaxation

This breathwork practice is designed for you to cultivate a deep sense of relaxation and loving support while sitting back to back. As you embark on this journey together, let your breath become a bridge, connecting you both on a profound level. This practice will help you synchronise your energies and create a tranquil space for mutual healing and connection.

### Setting the Scene
Create a quiet, comfortable space where you won't be disturbed. Place two cushions or pillows on the floor, one for each of you to sit on. Sit with your backs touching, forming a heartwarming connection.

### Posture
Sit in a comfortable cross-legged position with your hands resting on your knees, palms up. Close your eyes, and take a few moments to settle into your shared space. Take a few deep breaths and become aware of your partner's back touching yours.

### The Practice:

### Connecting Breaths (5 minutes).
- Start by taking a few deep breaths together. Inhale through your nose, allowing your abdomen to rise, and exhale gently through your mouth, releasing any tension.
- Now, focus on synchronising your breath with your partner's. As you breathe in, feel their breath moving your back, and as you breathe out, send your breath gently into their back.
- Continue this synchronised breathing, gradually finding a harmonious rhythm. Let go of any need to control the breath and simply allow it to flow naturally between the two of you.

### Heart-Centered Breath (5 minutes).
- Shift your focus to your heart centre. Imagine a radiant light at the centre of your chest, slowly expanding and filling your entire being with warmth and love. You may prefer the imagery of a many petaled flower opening with each inhalation and softly furling in on itself with each exhalation.

- As you inhale, visualise this light growing brighter and warmer. With each exhale, send this loving energy to your partner. Feel the reciprocity of their love and support flowing into you.

### Letting Go (5 minutes).
- Now, shift your awareness to any tension or worries you may be holding onto. As you breathe in, imagine these concerns as dark smoke.
- With each exhale, release this smoke into the earth, knowing that you are supported by your partner's presence and love. Feel the lightness that comes with letting go of these burdens.

### Unity Breath (5 minutes).
- As you continue breathing together, start to envision your breath as a bridge between your souls. With each inhale, imagine your energy intertwining, like the roots of two trees merging beneath the earth.
- As you exhale, picture this connection strengthening, creating a sense of profound unity and mutual support. You are two souls entwined, breathing as one.

### Gratitude and Affirmation (3 minutes).
- Take a few moments to express gratitude for this shared experience. Relax and rest your head back on your partner's shoulder. You can silently or verbally acknowledge what you appreciate about your partner and the connection you've nurtured.
- Offer words of appreciation to each other. Speak from the heart, reinforcing the love and support you feel in this moment.

### Closing and Embrace (2 minutes).
- Gently bring your focus back to your physical connection, your backs touching, your breath flowing freely.
- Embrace the feeling of support that your partner provides, both physically and emotionally. Hold this sensation close to your heart.
- Turn towards one another and hold each other tenderly for as long as feels appropriate.

This breathwork practice is a beautiful way for you to relax your nervous system and foster a profound sense of loving support. It allows you to connect on a deeper level, creating a shared space of healing, relaxation, and connection. Remember to communicate openly with your partner about your experiences during and after the practice, reinforcing your bond and understanding of each other.

Close the space with a quiet loving presence.

# 02

## Eye Gazing
### Soul to soul

Eye gazing is a profound practice involving sustained eye contact with your partner, free from distractions and words. It finds its place in spiritual and personal growth realms, offering an array of benefits for both individuals and relationships. To begin, choose a partner who is open and willing to partake in this practice, and set an intention—whether to strengthen your connection, enhance communication, or embrace the present moment.

Eye gazing fosters deeper connection and intimacy. Through prolonged eye contact, you can glimpse the true essence of your partner and establish a profound, authentic bond. This practice also refines communication. Eye gazing can also amplify self-awareness. As you softly gaze into another's eyes, you'll also reflect on your own feelings and emotions, offering valuable insights into your inner self. Moreover, eye gazing is a spiritual tool. It deepens one's practice by facilitating a connection with the divine within oneself and others, with the potential to be a potent and transformative experience.

### Eye Gazing Practice:

#### Set the Scene
Create a quiet and comfortable space to practice.
Choose a location where you won't be disturbed, and where you and your partner can sit facing each other comfortably.

#### Set a timer
It's helpful to set a timer for a predetermined amount of time, such as one minute, three minutes, or five minutes. Start slowly, you can build the length of time as you progress with regular practice. Consistency is the key to making integrated change.

#### To practice
- Sit facing each other, and take a few deep breaths before making soft eye contact.
- Gaze softly into one another's left eye.
- Try to maintain this eye contact without breaking it, even if it feels uncomfortable or awkward at first.

Eye gazing is a potent and revealing practice that may stir various thoughts and emotions. While it can be challenging, it offers deep insight. Initially, most of us shy away from allowing someone to peer into our souls through prolonged eye contact.

Start gently, with short sessions lasting just a minute or two, and gradually extend the duration with each practice, aiming for up to an hour of this profound open-hearted connection. You might feel challenged, tempted to look away, blink, or even giggle. Tears may flow as suppressed emotions surface in this non-judgmental engagement with your loved one.

Stay open, compassionate, and curious about your own and your partner's experiences.

### Reflection
After practice, take a moment to discuss your experience with your beloved. Share what you observed about your partner and the insights you gained about yourself.

Keep in mind that eye gazing can significantly deepen your connection with others and enhance your self-awareness. Approach it with an open heart and a willingness to be vulnerable, and you'll unlock its transformative potential.

Consciously close your practice time.

### In Practice:

I remember being in a soulful state of deep connection during an eye-gazing practice on a course many years ago. It was a profound practice, one that felt only moments in duration. We were surprised that we had been immersed in the experience far longer than intended. It was an intensely beautiful, moving, and stirring experience. We emerged long after the other course attendees had finished and packed up. During that particular eye gazing session (I have had many similar experiences since), I was moved to see and feel the shifting emotions within myself and my partner as we vulnerably remained present. I witnessed my partner shift from being a young girl through every stage of her life into an old and wise woman. It was like seeing through the masks and states and phases that she wore throughout her life. I felt deeply connected to her essence throughout. When we finished practice, we were giddy and deeply moved by the experience.

# 03

## Toroidal Breathing
### The breath of the Universe

The Toroidal Breathing Technique is a type of breathing exercise that involves visualising the flow of energy in and out of the body in a toroidal (doughnut-like, figure of eight) shape. It can be done alone or with a partner and has several potential benefits.

When practised with a partner, the Toroidal Breathing Technique can help to deepen the connection and trust between the two individuals. The exercise involves synchronising the breath with the partner, which can create a sense of unity and shared experience.

I have practised toroidal breathing many times in both intimate relationships and with partners, friends and students. It is a powerful and deeply nourishing practice, allowing one to experience feeling both connected, supported, and accepted as we learn to harmonise with another as one unified force of love.

In addition to the relational benefits, the circular, flowing movement of breath can help calm the mind and body, reducing stress and anxiety.

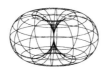

### Toroidal Breathing Technique with a Partner:
- Set a timer for 5 or 10 minutes.
- Sit or stand facing each other, with a comfortable distance between you.
- Begin by taking a few deep breaths together, inhaling through the nose and exhaling through the mouth.
- Visualise a toroidal shape through, and around your body. See diagram.
- Inhaling raise the hands up the front of the body to the heart centre, and pause.
- Exhale the hands above the head, keeping relaxed.

- Inhale as you softly draw your arms out to the sides - pause at shoulder height.
- Exhale the hands down towards the hips.

**You can explore practising this with reverse movements.**
- Inhale hands out to the sides of the body.
- Exhale hands above the head.
- Inhale hands down the central channel to the heart centre.
- Exhale hands down towards the hips.
- After 5 or 10 minutes of practice, share your experience with your partner.

Close the practice space with loving intention.

The Toroidal Breathing Technique with a partner can be a powerful tool for deepening relationships, reducing stress, and developing presence and focus. You may also find that you become more energetically attuned to yourself and your partner along with the subtle realms. It can be practised daily for increased potency.

# 04

## The Embrace of Tender Holding
### Sacred Union and Exquisite Polarity

Sacred Union and Exquisite Polarity: The Embrace of Tender Holding is a practice that transcends the physical, inviting you to explore the spiritual essence of your partnership. Through this beautiful ritual, you nurture a profound understanding of the energies that flow between you, forging a connection deeply rooted in trust and surrender. As you explore the sensations coursing through your bodies and souls, you embark on a shared journey of self-discovery, mutual growth, and love that is both transcendent and intimately grounded in the present moment.

### The Embrace of Tender Holding
To practice, prepare the sacred space and decide who will be actively holding and which one of you will be held. You can switch and experience the opposite position next time you practice. For now, one of you embodies the masculine frame of presence, and the other is being held in the feminine softness of receiving.

### Setting your Intention
- Set a time for your practice – aim for 10 to 20 minutes.
- Sit in a comfortable and relaxed manner, your legs entwined, creating a physical connection that mirrors your emotional bond.

### Centering Breath
- Close your eyes and take full breaths. Inhaling and exhaling release tension and worldly concerns.

### The Loving Embrace
- The partner who will be holding their beloved cradles them gently but firmly, creating a cocoon of safety.
- The one being held relaxes back into the embrace, surrendering to the support of their partner's loving arms and experiencing the weight of their legs wrapped around them.

### Intentional Holding
- The partner who is doing the holding places their hands around their partner, offering reassurance and love. The holding conveys profound tenderness, affection, and a deep commitment to providing an emotional refuge.

### Noticing the Sensations
- The partner being held closes their eyes, allowing your awareness to turn inwards.
- They focus on the sensations awakening within their body.
- Acknowledge the soothing warmth of their touch, the subtle rise and fall of their breath, and the energy that flows between you both.

### Vocalising Sensations
- Tune into your experience both physically, emotionally, mentally and energetically.
- Verbalise your experience as you relax into your beloved's embrace. For example, I feel a deep sense of security and love in your arms. I sense a profound peace. My heart feels heavy. I feel held, or I feel your presence. My heart feels full. I feel tension in my upper body. I feel numb. My heart is beating fast. I feel hot/cold/burdened/troubled/safe/resistant/soft. I enjoy the sensation of our bodies connecting.

Articulate your experience as clearly as possible, sharing your thoughts and feelings as they arise and pass. There is no right or wrong – simply an experience of this moment. Recognise any feelings of resistance, closure, or wanting to withhold your experience. Soften your heart and continue.

### Listening and Receiving
- The holding partner: As you share in your lover's experience, open your heart to receive your partner's words with love and receptivity.
- Encourage your beloved to express the sensations and emotions they are experiencing as they hold you. Do so without judgement or preconceived ideas about what the experience should be like. Don't take anything to heart – this is not about you.

After 10 to 20 minutes of practice:

### Deepening the Connection
- Let go of all that's been shared. Allow your breaths to synchronise, deepening your connection beyond the physical realm.
- Feel the exquisite polarity of your energies, a dance of masculine holding and feminine receptive responsiveness, yin and yang, in perfect harmony. Release the constraints of time and external distractions. In this moment, there is only you, your partner, and the profound connection you share.
- Continue this practice for as long as it feels natural, allowing your hearts to merge in a sacred union. Trust. You will know when to move into the next experience. Be patient and compassionate with one another.

### Concluding the Practice
- When the time feels right, slowly release your hold and open your eyes.
- Gaze into your loved one's eyes with gratitude, acknowledging the depth of connection you created.

Consciously close the space.

# 05

## Sacred Communication
The gift of conscious communication.

Conscious communication is a powerful practice that can help to strengthen the connection between partners and deepen intimacy. By practising active listening, using "I" statements, expressing gratitude, and incorporating touch, you can create a loving and connected relationship. This is especially useful after conflict or at times when you feel your needs are not being met.

### Conscious communication practice:

### Set an intention
Begin by setting an intention for your communication practice. This could be to deepen intimacy, resolve a conflict, or simply connect more deeply with your partner. Create a loving container to practice.

### Connect with your partner
Take a moment to connect with your partner before beginning the practice. This could involve holding hands, sitting close together, or simply making eye contact.

### Express gratitude
Take time to express gratitude for your partner and the things they do that you appreciate. This can help to create a positive and loving atmosphere.

### Practice active listening
One of the key components of conscious communication is active listening. This involves being fully present and attentive to your partner as they speak, without interrupting or judging them. Listen with your whole body to understand and not to correct the other. Use "I" statements: Instead of blaming or criticising your partner, use "I" statements to express how you feel. For example, instead of saying "You never listen to me," say "I feel unheard when I try to talk to you."

### Practice touch
Conscious communication often involves touch as a way of deepening intimacy and connection. This could involve holding hands, hugging, or simply touching each other's arms or shoulders. Close the sharing time lovingly.

---

# 06

## Life by Design – Shared values
Birth a new vision for what is possible.

Choosing shared values is a profound way to deepen your relationship and enhance your connection. When you align on values, you'll feel more understood and supported by your partner. These chosen values serve as your Relational North Star, guiding your decisions and keeping you on track, especially when your relationship faces challenges.

Remember, the meaning of things is what we give them. Values are the emotional expression we want to experience in life. By consciously selecting your values, you wield the power to transform your relationship and life as a whole. Values are the core beliefs that shape your priorities, often operating beneath your awareness. By bringing them to the forefront of your decisions, you gain a potent tool for nurturing your relationship's growth and alignment with your shared vision.

Life is a constant juggle of values—balancing personal needs with the needs of others in areas like finances, family, relationships, travel, and personal growth. Working through values conflicts as a couple helps you to clarify your shared values. Focusing your awareness on them becomes the foundation for sound decision-making. This approach ensures you stay true to your course and evolve your values and relationships as you individuate and grow together.

Consciously creating and designing your relationship means taking an active and intentional approach to how you relate to your partner. It involves defining what you want from the relationship, setting goals and priorities, and working with your partner to achieve them.

The benefits of consciously creating and designing your relationship are many. By taking an active approach, you can build a relationship that is fulfilling, satisfying, and aligned with your values and priorities. It can also help you build trust, intimacy, and emotional connection with your partner. Remember that you are on each other's side, not against each other and birthing a new vision for what is possible will support you in being better equipped to handle them together when the inevitable challenges arise.

Here are 10 relationship-enhancing values to consider:

**Communication:** Open and honest dialogue fosters understanding and trust.
**Respect:** Treating each other with dignity and kindness is essential.
**Quality Time:** Prioritise spending meaningful moments together.
**Trust:** Build a foundation of reliability and faith in one another.
**Empathy:** Show compassion and understanding for each other's feelings.
**Love:** Choosing love supports you in being open to relational growth.
**Connection:** Fostering a deep sense of connection facilitates certainty and dependability.
**Adaptability:** Be open to change and adapt as your relationship evolves.
**Support:** Offer encouragement and help each other in times of need.
**Equality:** Ensure fairness and balance in the relationship.

By consciously choosing your values, you'll have a powerful guide for decision-making and maintain alignment with your relational truth. Recognise that life often presents you with conflicts between values but when you prioritise your shared values as a couple, you'll stay on course and evolve together as individuals and partners. Remember, you have the time, energy, motivation, and effort to invest in what you value most, and these values will be the driving force behind your relationship's growth and fulfilment.

## Life by Design: Shared Values Practice

### Here are some tips for choosing values as a couple:

#### Communicate openly
Start by talking about what values are important to you individually. Share your values and what they mean to you. Then, listen to your partner's values without judgment. This will help you understand each other's perspectives and create a foundation for choosing shared values.

#### Identify shared values
Look for values that you agree on or those that are similar to each other's values. Some values that couples often share are honesty, respect, trust, communication, commitment, and kindness. However, there could be many more that are important to you both.

#### Ends Values
Identify values used to meet other needs. These are vehicles or means values. For example, family, work, hobbies, and wealth. These inherently have numerous values built into them that represent our desires and what we value most.

#### Prioritise values
Once you've identified shared values, map them out and prioritise them in order of importance. This will help you focus on the most meaningful values..

#### Create a shared vision
Use your shared values to create a vision for your relationship. Discuss what your shared values mean to you and how you can integrate them into your daily life. This will help to deepen your connection and build a strong foundation for your

relationship.

### Revisit your shared values regularly
As your relationship evolves, so might your values. Make it a point to revisit your shared values regularly and discuss any changes or adjustments that need to be made.

Choosing values as a couple is not about compromising or sacrificing your needs. It's about finding common ground and creating a shared vision that supports both of you in your relationship. Re-committing to chosen values of relating together may guide you in transforming the hurts of the past into wisdom.

Top Tip:

For maximum effect weigh all of your decisions upon your chosen values. If the choices you have to make steer you towards your life vision and the love you wish to embody then it is a yes. If the decision you are pondering takes you away from your vision and doesn't align with your values it's a no. Your choices in every moment determine the unfolding of your life. In the same manner, your previous decisions created the current circumstances of your life.

Ask yourself does this decision/choice take me closer to god/love/my life vision? If not walk away and choose again.

# 07

# Keep the Spark Alive!
## The Sacred Art of Solitude and Honouring Time Apart

In the intricate dance of love and intimacy, one might think that togetherness is the ultimate goal. However, if we delve deeper into the realm of conscious relationships, we find that the space between two lovers is just as crucial as the connection itself.

It is imperative to the health of your relationship with yourself and your lover to explore the profound significance of having time apart to pursue personal pleasures, passions, hobbies, and moments of solitude. In turn, these moments apart may well bring a greater frisson of excitement, interest and polarity to the flow of your relationship as you lean into intrigue and curiosity as to who your loved one is beyond your togetherness.

### The beauty of individuality
Imagine a garden where every flower is unique, each possessing its own distinctive fragrance, colour, and beauty. In the same way, individuals within a relationship are like the diverse blooms in that garden. While the togetherness of the garden is undoubtedly enchanting, it is equally important to allow each flower to bask in the sunlight of its individuality.

### Nurturing self-growth
Personal growth is an integral part of any conscious relationship. When partners take time apart to pursue their passions and hobbies, they nurture their growth. This self-nourishment is not selfish but rather self-full, and essential for the blossoming of the relationship itself. It is in these moments of individual exploration that we gain new skills, knowledge, and experiences to enrich our connection with our loved ones.

### Rekindling desire
Absence, as they say, makes the heart grow fonder. Spending time apart can reignite the flames of desire within a relationship. When partners reunite after pursuing their own passions and interests, they often bring back a renewed sense of excitement and appreciation for one another. The longing and anticipation that arise during these separations can breathe fresh life into a partnership.

### Fostering Independence

A conscious relationship is not about two halves making a whole. It is about two whole individuals coming together. Spending time alone allows partners to maintain their independence and self-sufficiency. It empowers each person to continue growing as an individual whilst simultaneously contributing to the growth of the relationship. This lends itself to developing a healthy interdependence.

### Cultivating Trust

Trust is the bedrock of any lasting relationship. Allowing your partner the freedom to explore their interests and passions demonstrates a deep trust in their commitment to the relationship. When both individuals trust each other's need for personal time, the bond between them becomes even stronger. If you find yourself experiencing feelings of anxiety about your lover's time apart, this is your invitation to lean in and strengthen yourself emotionally.

### Embracing the Practice of Solitude

Solitude is a gift you give to yourself. It's a time for self-reflection, rejuvenation, and inner exploration. When you cherish moments of solitude, you become more in touch with your desires, dreams, and values. This self-awareness enhances your personal growth and enriches your interactions with your loved ones.

In the play of your relationship, the threads of togetherness and apartness are woven together to create a harmonious and resilient bond. The pursuit of personal passions, hobbies, and time alone does not need to be a threat to intimacy. It, instead, is a testament to the depth and strength of the connection between two individuals. By recognising the importance of time apart, we embrace the profound truth that love is not about possession but celebration, growth, and choice.

Taking time apart may look like having hobbies and activities outside of the relationship, going on retreat, going for daily walks, hiking or a regular form of exercise. It may look like having a daily spiritual practice or meditation practice to drop into and know yourself more clearly.

Create a dynamic within your relationship where you can actively request time apart and be rewarded for your openness, honesty, and integrity without fear, resistance or resentment.

# 08

## Exploring Sensation Practice
Polarity, the play of love and resting in oneness.

There are many ways to come back to the centre together and create moments of harmony, acceptance, and deep communication by exploring your and your partner's parameters for intimacy, connection, and growth. These moments and practices will support you as you turn towards each other, again and again.

The following practice is to support you in developing sacred touch, communication, and presence with one another.

### Exploring Sensation Practice

### Setting the scene
Choose a cosy and private space where you and your partner can relax without distractions. Make sure it's a place that allows you to fully immerse yourselves in this experience by creating a soft, warm, and intimate atmosphere. Play gentle, soothing music in the background to create a relaxing ambience. You may require a cushion to sit on and have two washcloths to hand. Wear clothes that reveal the length of your arms and that you wouldn't mind getting a little oil on. Set a clear intention to be loving, open, and curious before commencing.

### Prepare some oil
Use sweet almond or fractionated coconut oil and place it within easy reach. You could gently warm the oil by placing the bottle of oil in a bowl of hot water.

### To begin
- Sit cross-legged facing each other. Have your knees almost touching one another.
- Connect with a few words of gratitude some deep breaths, and a hug. Allow your awareness to drift freely, then draw it into the room - into your private chamber.

### Practice Eye Gazing for 3 - 5 mins (refer to Chapter 2, page 64).
- Share your experience with open and clear dialogue.
- As one of you shares, the other holds space by remaining present and open-hearted without making any comments. Receive your partner's words acceptingly.
- Let your partner know you're interested in hearing more. Ask questions like, 'Is

there anything else on your mind?' or 'What else would you like me to know?'

Remember, there is no right or wrong way to express yourself. Stay present and attentive, and if you find yourself getting distracted or uneasy, take a moment to refocus. When it is your turn, share your experiences in a similar open and honest manner.

### Exploring Sensation Practice
This practice is designed to help you distinguish between various types of touch and foster emotional, energetic, and physical connection. This is a valuable tool to explore how your partner receives different qualities of touch.

### The four qualities are:
Holding Touch
Healing Touch
Sensual Touch
Erotic Touch

### First of all, you will be exploring Holding Touch.
There will be a giver and a receiver. Decide who will go first.
You, as the 'giver', will be oiling your partner's forearm using different qualities of touch. Be intentional and give yourself a moment to tap into the quality you are exploring.

- Relaxed, the receiver sits with their arm uncovered and resting in their lap.
- Place some warm oil in the palm of your hand.
- Tune into the quality you are exploring, in this case, Holding Touch.
- Gently but firmly take your partner's hand. You may cradle their forearm or hold it comfortably, perhaps at the elbow.
- Start to gently soothe the oil over your partner's forearm, massaging, holding, and oiling in a manner that, to you, represents Holding Touch. Be intentional, present and relaxed. Notice if you feel distracted, then bring yourself back to presence.
- Continue for a few minutes. Observe your partner's responses.
- Rest your partner's arm back in their lap. Take a few deep breaths together.
- Your partner will now share their experience with you. Do not make comments. Listen. Receive. Learn.

Now switch. You become the receiver and your partner the giver. Follow the same oiling process for Holding Touch, then share your experience of receiving Holding Touch.

Repeat this process for each of the qualities: Holding Touch, Healing Touch, Sensual Touch, and Erotic Touch, in turn. Take your time. There is no rush and no agenda. When you have completed the practice with each of the four qualities, share your overall experience. Share which kind of touch you enjoyed or needed most and why.

This powerful practice helps you to foster presence, energetic and emotional openness, and the sacred gift of intentional touch.

Close the space and practice time lovingly, with appreciation for all you have shared.

# 09

## Sacred Bathing Ritual

Devotion is sexy. What are you devoting your life to?

### Sacred Bathing Ritual:

### Setting the Scene

Choose a cosy and private space where you and your partner can relax without distractions. Whether it's a cabin in the mountains or a room at home, make sure it's a place that allows you to immerse yourselves in this sacred experience.

Light a fire and candles to create a soft, warm, and intimate atmosphere. Lay cosy blankets and a bath sheet on the floor. Prepare a basin of water at the perfect temperature. Add a drop or two of your favourite essential oil to the water and place it within easy reach. Place fluffy towels and robes nearby, ensuring your partner's comfort before and after the ritual. Play gentle, soothing music in the background to create an ambience of love and tenderness.

### The Sacred Bathing Ritual

- Begin by sitting across from each other in front of a fireplace or an altar of candles. Take a few moments to connect through eye contact, holding hands, or even a loving embrace.
- Set your intention for this ritual: to nurture, tend to, celebrate, and deeply connect with your partner.
- As the one holding space, express your appreciation and admiration for your partner. remind them that this is a time for unconditional love and acceptance.
- Invite your partner to undress and lay on the blankets. Cover your partner in a soft blanket or sheet.
- Using a soft cloth, gently start bathing your partner, beginning with their head and face. Use tender strokes and loving attention. Your unwavering presence and appreciation are key to this being a magical experience for you both. As you tend your partner be aware of how incredible they are and how amazing their body is. Be appreciative of all this person you love has been through.
- As you wash your beloved maintain a connection through your gaze and touch. Let your love and appreciation flow through your hands.
- Continue bathing your partner, moving down to their neck and shoulders. Use the water, essential oils, and cloth to cleanse and relax their muscles.

- Pay attention to any areas that might carry tension and lovingly release it.
- If you both feel comfortable, gradually move down to bathe the rest of their body. Take your time, savouring each moment and appreciating the beauty of their form, speaking words of love, admiration, and gratitude as you go along.

Encourage your partner to surrender to the experience, allowing them to receive your care and affection. Remember to be present, attentive, and sensitive to their needs and desires.

- As the ritual comes to a close, wrap them in a fluffy towel or robe to keep them warm and cocooned in your love.
- Take a moment to hold each other close, appreciating the depth of connection and intimacy you've shared.
- Share any reflections or feelings that arose during the ritual.

Allow yourselves to bask in the afterglow of this sacred experience. You may choose to rest by the fire, cuddle, or simply be in each other's presence, savouring the love that surrounds you.

If bathing the entire body feels too much at first, you can start with the hands and feet. Then when you feel comfortable, bathe the head, neck and face. There is no rush. Go at your and your partner's own rate and respond to your sense of readiness for this intimacy practice. The key is to create an environment of loving trust and comfort.

### Sacred Body Oiling
You may wish to enhance the Sacred Bathing Ritual with body oiling.

To practice: Use a nourishing massage oil to further connect with your partner's body, allowing your hands to glide over their skin with tenderness and care.

Remember that the Sacred Bathing Ritual is a profound act of love and connection. It's about creating a space where you and your partner can feel cherished, accepted, and deeply connected. Keep your presence and unwavering attention at the centre of this beautiful experience, be mindful of the vulnerability your partner may be experiencing, and let it strengthen the bonds of love between you and your beloved.

Close the space with loving attention.

# 10

## Beyond the trigger, an open heart
### The simple key to your transformation

Our relationships can have moments where we find ourselves charged when conflict and upsets occur. This may result in us pointing our finger at the 'other' as the source of our discomfort and suffering. These judgements may help us momentarily shift focus from ourselves and any feelings of confusion, anger, and upset we may be experiencing, but will, over time, hold us back from being the love we truly desire. In judging the other, we keep our power at bay, creating a fracture of separation within ourselves.

**Ask yourself:** Do I habitually block suffering rather than assimilate it? When I let myself experience any internal resistance or upset, how can I support myself? What would change if I allowed myself to fully feel and express myself when hurt, angered, upset, sad, or grieving? Who would I be, and how would I show up?

If you find yourself dissociating, avoiding, or dismissing after an upset for fear of suffering, what do you hope to achieve by doing so? What does this mean for you long-term? What could be different if you were willing to face what you habitually turn away from or resist?

### Solo Transmutation Practice to Embrace Love

This practice will support you in calling power back to yourself by integrating and transmuting discord from within so that you may take radical responsibility for how you are showing up and for the circumstances of your relationship—as a gift to yourself and your loved ones. You may use this practice when you feel upset or to help you understand and discharge a particular pattern you experience repeatedly.

### The Seduction of Separation

- Find a comfortable space where you can be uninterrupted.
- Close your eyes and take a few deep breaths, allowing your body to relax and your mind to settle. With practice, you will be able to do this practice on the go.
- Bring your awareness to the sensations in your body. There may be anger, fear, resistance, or judgment. Don't resist or judge. Simply acknowledge this presence and let go of the need to analyse or create stories around your experience.
- Sink into the very core of the sensations as if you're melting into their embrace.
- Allow yourself to be fully present with what you're feeling.

- This part of you that feels resistant, separate from love, or hurt has an identity alive from within you.
- There is no need to reject this part of you that feels separate. It simply needs loving presence and acceptance.

**Enquire:** Where is this feeling or energy located in my body? Does it have a colour? Texture? Temperature? How big or small is it? What does it want me to know? What messages does it have for me? Be present, curious, and stay in the sensation for as long as required - feeling it through you. Trust your experience, allowing these messages and the identity of this energetic imprint to reveal itself to you.

## Embracing Love
There is another part of you that knows the truth that there is only love and connection and that all is well.

- Gently bring your awareness to the part of you that knows there is no separation. Locate this truth as a sensation in your body. It may be love, peace, or connection. Simply acknowledge this presence. Let go of the need to analyse or create stories around your experience.
- Sink into the very core of these sensations, as if you are melting into its embrace. Allow yourself to be fully present with what you're feeling.
- This part of you that knows love and connection has an identity alive within you.

**Enquire:** Where is this connection to all that is located in my body? Where is the energy of love located in my body? Does it have a colour? Texture? Temperature? How big or small is it? What does it want me to know? What messages does it have for me? Be present, curious, and stay in the sensation for as long as required—feeling it all of the way through.

- What does this part of you that knows love and connection want the part that feels disconnected or separate to know? What message does the presence of connection and love have for the part alive within you that is in separation?
- Now, allow this loving energy and message to bathe the wounded separate part of you.
- Let the colour of love bathe that part of you that is in separation consciousness with its tender and potent messages of love and acceptance—saturating it in love.
- Visualise this or speak it aloud. You may place your hands upon your body, demonstrating where this integration occurs. You may visualise this as vibrant currents of light.
- Breathe deeply. Rest. Allow this process to be complete.
- Feel the energies shifting within you.
- Take a few more deep breaths, and feel your intention be integrated and settle within you. When you're ready, gently open your eyes, carrying this sense of love and connection into the world of possibility.

Remember: This practice is a gift you can offer yourself whenever you feel challenged or triggered. Embrace it as a ritual of love—knowing that you hold the keys to your transformation.

# 11

## For Him. I am. That I Am
Meditation will change your life

The benefits of adopting a regular meditation practice are well-documented and innumerable. Perhaps you are already exploring meditation as a healthy practice within the context of your daily life. If you have not yet committed to a daily meditation practice, this is your opportunity to do so! As a masculine consciousness being, meditation is your ideal practice to develop your capacity to be fully present, with an open heart and a clear energetic channel. The personal benefits you will gain by practising for even as little as twenty minutes a day will enhance how you show up for your work and your relationships. Developing presence through meditation is an incredible way to reduce stress, increase awareness, and improve overall well-being. Here's a simple guided meditation practice to help you cultivate presence:

### Becoming Present Meditation:
You can start with 5-10 minutes and gradually increase the practice time to 20 minutes as you become more comfortable.

### To practice
- Find a quiet and comfortable place to sit. You can use a cushion or a chair, whichever you find more comfortable.
- Set a timer for 5, 10 or 20 minutes.
- Sit with your back straight and your hands resting on your lap or knees. Close your eyes to minimise external distractions.

### Focus on Your Breath
- Begin by taking a few deep breaths in through your nose and exhaling slowly through your mouth. This will help you relax.
- Notice the sounds around you, whether they are distant or nearby. Allow them to come and go without getting caught up in them.
- Allow your breath to return to its natural rhythm.
- Shift your attention to the sensation of your breath as it enters and leaves your nostrils. Feel the coolness of the inhalation and the warmth of the exhalation.

### I am. That I Am
- With each breath allow the mantra 'I am. That I Am' to loosely reverberate

around you, breathing and repeating 'I am. That I Am.' for the duration of your meditation.

- Inhaling 'I am.' Exhaling 'That I Am.'

## End the Practice
- Let the mantra go.
- Feel the sensations in your body, from the contact between your body and the chair or cushion to any other physical sensations.
- When you're ready, gently open your eyes and take a few deep breaths. Stretch your body if needed, and carry the sense of presence and calm with you into your day.

## Gratitude and Positive Intention
As you conclude your meditation, take a moment to express gratitude for this time you've dedicated to yourself.
- Set a positive intention for the day or the next steps in your life. This could be a simple affirmation or a specific goal.

## Acceptance and Non-Judgment
If your mind becomes busy with thoughts, don't be critical of yourself. Instead, acknowledge the thoughts and gently guide your attention back to your breath or the present moment. Remember that the goal is not to eliminate thoughts but to observe them without attachment.

Remember, developing presence takes time and practice. Be patient with yourself and make meditation a regular part of your day. Over time, you'll find that you become more grounded and present in your everyday life.

### In practice:

Having collaborated with numerous individuals over the years who have grappled with the challenge of balancing work, home life, and the need for personal space, all while cultivating connections with other individuals. Achieving balance in this dynamic is undeniably difficult. A fulfilling and diverse life inevitably introduces a host of values conflicts. My advice, based on my experiences with these individuals, is to regularly align yourself with the truth in your heart. Establish clear boundaries around elements that may divert you from your path, and ensure that you allocate time for self-reflection, akin to retreating into the 'cave.' This period serves as crucial processing, decision-making, and realignment with your life's mission. Despite potential objections from your partner, maintaining a steadfast and loving demeanour while articulating specific times available for connection will ultimately establish you as a leader. The key lies in curating time to delve into your inner self, recognising your needs, and then integrating this self-awareness into the fabric of your relationships. This proactive approach allows you, your partner, and your family to not only thrive but also witness the emergence of your best self.

## The power of honing a practical skill

Harnessing the power of honing a practical skill extends beyond its immediate benefits, serving as a potent tool for cultivating and embodying masculine presence. An effective strategy to foster this development involves engaging in a new sport, activity, or hobby that demands your undivided attention and commitment. Whether it's the rugged terrain of hiking, the camaraderie of team sports, the strategic challenges of climbing, the rhythmic enjoyment of cycling, the immersive experience of swimming, the craftsmanship of woodworking, or any other pursuit that thrusts you into the realm of the unfamiliar, the key lies in becoming a beginner once again.

Embracing a novel endeavour not only necessitates the acquisition of new skills but also invites you to navigate the often uncomfortable space between your current abilities and the mastery you aspire to achieve. This process propels personal growth by compelling you to confront your edges, fostering resilience, and anchoring you to a clear intention. As you grapple with the learning curve, you develop a profound understanding of commitment, patience, and perseverance.

Beyond the immediate advantages of skill acquisition, dedicating time to a new pursuit provides a valuable respite from the demands of everyday life. This intentional separation allows for moments of introspection, enabling you to recalibrate and reconnect with your inner self. It becomes a sanctuary where you can detach from the immediacies of home life, offering a necessary pause to reflect on your journey and aspirations.

This deliberate pursuit of a practical skill also enhances your capacity to embody qualities of presence—a gift that extends beyond personal development. As you navigate the challenges of your chosen activity, you bring newfound depth and mindfulness to your interactions, including those within your intimate relationships. The skills honed in your chosen pursuit become a testament to your dedication, translating into a more grounded and resilient approach to both your personal growth and the dynamics of love.

In essence, the journey of mastering a practical skill becomes a transformative process, shaping not only your abilities in a specific domain but also enriching your character and fortifying your masculine presence. It is a holistic endeavour that intertwines personal development, commitment, resilience, and the ability to offer the gift of presence to those you cherish.

# 12

## For Her. I Feel
### Move to the rhythm of your emotions

Awakening the heart and feminine sensuality involves a deep exploration of one's inner self and connection with the divine energy within. By embracing all aspects of the self, including the sensual, erotic, dark, and emotional, you awaken your capacity to feel and express that which is closest to the womb of your heart. The path of awakening your body and feminine sensuality is deeply personal. It will require your commitment, compassion, and rawness. Please approach the following practices with openness, playful curiosity, and a commitment to your growth and self-discovery. It can be a transformative journey that leads to greater self-acceptance, love, and connection with your inner feminine essence.

**I feel. Move to the rhythm of your emotions.**
Embrace the cosmic flow of love coursing through your very being. Feel it as it awakens, stirs, and surges within you. Let it move through your body—a primordial dance.

**To practice:**
Create a beautiful private space to be with yourself. See the Opening Ritual on p. for inspiration. Choose music that takes you on a journey of sensual and erotic discovery. Be playful with your musical choices—jungle beats, soulful serenades, jazz, music that makes you want to move. Dress yourself in beautiful clothes and adorn yourself—be naked if you prefer. Wear your favourite scent and light candles.

**Shaking**
Let loose, and liberate your life force energy. Stand with your feet hip-width apart and gently connect with your breath, body, and heart. Start to shake your whole body in a freeing, non-linear manner. Shake, bounce and loosen all the pent-up energy that longs to be expressed.

**Circling**
Circle your hips as if drawing sacred circles in the sand. In this circular motion, find the rhythm of your existence— locate your heartbeat—move with it. Let it remind you that you are part of the eternal flow of love.

**Express**

Express yourself authentically. Vent the emotions you've held back, for emotions are the rivers through which love flows. Feel every nuance of your feelings without judgment, for they are the raw material of your feminine journey.

## Ground
Ground yourself like the roots of a mighty tree, for it is from this earthy foundation that you may bloom. Feel the stability beneath your feet, the solid support of the universal ground itself.

## Writhe
Writhe like the ocean waves crashing against the shore. Let your body move as it wishes, unencumbered by societal expectations. Free yourself from the constraints of perfection and allow your authenticity to shine through.

## Open
Open your hips, for they are the gateway to your heart and soul. Open hips—Open heart. Open your heart, for it is the centre of your divine being. In the union of open hips and an open heart, you will find a profound connection to the infinite love that surrounds you.

## Explore
Explore your edges and play with your emotional boundaries. It is at these edges that you will discover new facets of yourself and the infinite depths of love within.

## Free yourself
Free yourself from the habitual patterns of holding and withholding. Love flows freely, without conditions or reservations. Be an expression of overflowing love, let love flow.

## Liberate
Liberate yourself. Break free from the shackles of perfectionism and embrace your body, for she carries you in the light and the dark, a sacred home for your surrendered bliss.

## Shine
Let your heart shine like the full moon in the night sky. Let her guide you courageously. Intuitively. Freely.

## Sigh it out
Sigh it out, make sounds, release. The divine love within you is not meant to be contained or stifled. It longs to be expressed, to be heard, to be felt. To be penetrated.

## Embrace
Embrace the flow of love through you, for it is your birthright. Let it fill every fibre of your being, let it remind you that you are a divine and infinite expression of love itself.

## Deep Rest
After your practice lay down on soft blankets and let your whole body come into a state of deep stillness. Remain here for at least 10 - 20 minutes.

**Practices for you to explore and awaken your depth of feminine magnetism and awaken the heart of your feminine sensuality:**

**Sensory Exploration:**
Engage your senses to connect with your sensuality. Experiment with textures, tastes, scents, and sounds that evoke a sensual response. Be fully present and mindful in these experiences.

**Acceptance:**
Embracing all aspects of yourself, including any perceived flaws or insecurities. Loving yourself unconditionally is a powerful step towards awakening the heart and sensuality.

**Sacred Rituals:**
Create sacred rituals that honour your femininity and sensuality. Light candles, burn incense and set an intention to connect with your heart and sensuality during these rituals.

**Dancing:**
Put on music that makes you want to move your hips. Move your body unconsciously to the rhythm of your emotions. Express your sensuality, allowing your body to move intuitively. Liberate yourself, tap into the unbound childlike delight in your body. This practice can help you connect with your body's wisdom and sensuality.

**Womb and Heart Connection:**
Revere the womb as a sacred space. Self-massage and self-exploration can help you connect with your sensuality and deepen your understanding of your body. Connect to the energy of your womb space. Use natural oils like coconut oil for a gentle massage. This will support you even if you no longer have a physical womb.

**Affirmative Prayer:**
Daily prayer is a powerful way to connect with your deepest desires and align your life force energy with your intentions. Find powerful prayers here: https://bit.ly/46FmZ9q

**Yoni Steaming:**
A holistic practice involving steam treatments for the female reproductive system to promote physical and emotional well-being.

**Dry Body Brushing:**
Gently brush your skin with a dry brush to exfoliate, improve circulation, and stimulate the lymphatic system.

**Abhyanga:**
An Ayurvedic self-massage technique using warm oil to nourish and rejuvenate the body, promoting relaxation and balance.

**Singing and Chanting:**
Expressing oneself vocally, can bring you immense joy, release emotions, and promote a sense of inner connection as your cervix and throat are connected via your vagus nerve.

**Connecting with Mother Nature:**
Spending time immersed in the natural world to experience tranquillity, reduce stress, and enhance overall mental and physical health. This could include caring for plants and nurturing your outdoor space, which can provide a sense of fulfilment and tranquillity, whilst creating an inviting aura around your home.

**Dressing and Adorning Yourself:**
Choose clothing and accessories that make you feel confident and express your unique style and personality.

**Creating Your Own Signature Essential Oil Scent:**
Blending essential oils to craft a unique fragrance that suits your preferences and enhances your mood.

**Arranging Flowers and Beautifying Your Home:**
Engaging in creative activities like flower arranging to make your living space more aesthetically pleasing and harmonious, as you foster greater presence and openness.

**Deep Relaxation:**
Practising techniques like Yoga Nidra to induce a state of profound calm and stress relief.

**Gua Sha:**
A traditional Chinese facial and body treatment that involves scraping the skin with a smooth tool to improve circulation and promote healing.

### In practice:

It has been a great privilege to share these practices with clients, students, and friends over the years. In doing so, I have witnessed the power of women choosing to gift themselves self-care practices that deeply nourish them on a soul level whilst enlivening their feminine essence. This, in turn, becomes a gift of loving vitality to those around them. As a feminine being, you may find yourself putting others' needs before your own and worrying about being selfish for prioritising your well-being. This leads to burnout, loss of vitality, and resentment. Consider that filling your self-care cup to overflowing will provide you with the means to flourish as you care for and tend to those you love. This is a self-full act of love. Not a selfish act that takes away from others. This may fly in the face of the feminine conditioning you may have received of being in service to others before yourself. I urge you to challenge that assumption and give yourself the loving attention you desire.
Remember: self-care is more than skin deep, it includes doing your inner work to shift from fear, resistance and unhelpful patterns so that you thrive in all areas of your life.

## Breast Massage

Exploring the practice of breast massage serves as a profound pathway for fostering a deeper connection with your body, unlocking not only the potential for heart-centred openness but also the awakening of pleasure centres. Beyond its sensual dimensions, this mindful approach to self-care brings with it numerous physiological benefits by delicately stimulating lymph flow and drainage. Deliberate engagement with breast massage amplifies your sensitivity to touch, creating a harmonious intersection of physical and emotional well-being.

At its core, breast massage becomes a gateway to self-discovery and self-love. By intentionally directing attention and touch to this often-neglected part of the body, you can embark on a journey of reconnection with your feminine essence. This practice extends beyond the purely physical realm, becoming a holistic means of cultivating a positive body image and nurturing a sense of empowerment.

As you develop a weekly or daily breast massage practice, you will create a heightened sensitivity to touch, a perception of energy in your body and enhanced body awareness. This increased awareness contributes to a more profound connection with your body and extends to your intimate relationships, enriching the overall experience of touch and intimacy.

Approaching breast massage with the spirit of self-care transforms it into a loving ritual. It becomes an opportunity to honour and cherish your body, fostering a positive relationship with yourself. This intentional practice creates a space for you to tap into your sensuality, celebrating the unique and sacred aspects of your femininity.

In essence, embracing breast massage goes beyond the surface-level notions of self-care, evolving into a transformative practice that intertwines physical health, emotional well-being, and the celebration of your body. It is a journey of self-discovery, an avenue for pleasure, and a powerful act of love that extends far beyond the physical act.

### A Simple Breast Massage Practice:
Before you begin, find a quiet and comfortable space where you can relax without distractions. You may want to use a natural oil, such as coconut or almond oil, to facilitate smooth and gentle movements.

**Set the Mood:** Start by creating a calming atmosphere. Dim the lights, play soft music if you prefer, and ensure you won't be interrupted during your practice.

**Soft Breathing:** Take a few deep breaths to centre yourself and bring your awareness to the present moment. Inhale deeply through your nose, filling your lungs, and exhale slowly through your mouth, releasing any tension.

**Gentle Self-Check:** Begin by placing your hands over your heart and taking a moment to connect with yourself. This simple gesture helps ground you and establishes a connection between your heart and your breath.

**Warm-up:** Rub your hands together to generate warmth. Place your warm hands over your breasts without applying pressure. Take a few moments to appreciate the warmth transferring to your breast tissue.

**Circular Massaging Motion:** Using the pads of your fingers, start making gentle circular motions on your breasts. Begin from the centre and move up, outwards, and down around, covering the entire breast. Maintain a light touch, focusing on the sensation rather than pressure.
Repeat this motion 10 to 20 times.

**Energetic Stimulation:** Gently sweep your fingers from the centre, down and around your breasts towards the armpits, then up and to the centre again.
Repeat this motion 10 to 20 times.

**Heart-Centred Connection:** Gently cup your breasts, holding them gently but firmly. Feel their weight, and tune into any messages they have for you. Bring your attention to your heart centre. Visualise positive energy and love flowing from your heart to your breasts. This helps to cultivate a heart-centred connection and enhances the emotional aspect of the practice.

**Sensory Awareness:** Pay attention to the sensations in your breasts and the surrounding areas. Notice any areas of tension or tenderness, and adjust your massage accordingly. This practice is about cultivating awareness and self-compassion.

**Closing the Practice:** After 5-10 minutes of massage, place your hands over your heart once again, take a few deep breaths, and express gratitude for this time of self-care.

Remember, this practice is about creating a positive connection with your body and promoting a sense of well-being. Listen to your body, and feel free to modify the practice to suit your comfort and preferences. Make this a regular part of your self-care routine for lasting benefits.

# 13

## Putting it into practice
Creating a vision, purpose, and progress for
your developing relational intimacy

At the heart of any enduring and developing relational intimacy is knowing that no matter what, you both commit to and prioritise times of discovery and togetherness. As we discussed earlier in the book, the grass is always greener where you water it. If you want your relationship to evolve, and you and your partner along with it, it takes commitment, dedication and a shared purpose for your grand relational and life vision. Think of your relationship as an experiment, one that you are curious about and one that is sacred and sustaining. A relationship that is designed to change as you do, depending on your life phase.

Having regular check-ins to discuss the relationship, where your needs are being met and where improvement may be developed and scheduling regular date nights, couples retreats and times of separation are healthy components of a thriving continued commitment to your beloved.

Choosing your partner daily based on who they are now, rather than the memory of who they once were, is a vital aspect of any conscious relationship. This encourages interpersonal appreciation, curiosity, cooperation, and a desire to continue uncovering new layers of yourself and your partner.

The practices in this book have been designed to support you in deepening your connection to yourself and your lover. These practices and sacred rituals will evolve with you as you come closer and closer to the truth of who you are and cast off outdated identities to forge a way forward for your emergent self.

The decision to change is an in-the-moment choice. The process of change does not typically occur overnight. Lasting and meaningful transformation takes dedication and commitment. It takes you having a deeper meaning and values system as the basis of the shift you seek—with this in place, it will be easier for you to stay the course—even as it gets challenging and you come up against your internal resistance and perhaps resistance from those around you. Remember, others are used to you living, identifying and reacting differently and will need time to get used to who you are becoming.

## Consistency over perfection.

As you willingly show up time and time again for yourself, your loved ones, and the sacred container of your relationship, you will recognise moments of inner transformation reflected on the outer contours of your life. You will also learn to navigate plateaus, where it feels like the needle isn't moving forward, and perhaps, too, the odd slide backwards as you navigate change in a wholesome and integrative manner. All of this is normal and to be accepted and even celebrated. You are, after all, transforming yourself beyond the status quo, forging a new path for yourself and developing greater relational integrity.

Not everyone will understand what you are doing or why. If they did, they, too, would be embarking upon this quest for a radical shift in perspective and placing a more meaningful value system within the vehicle of their relationship. Keep on keeping on. Aim for consistency over perfection and tap into all the reasons you have embarked upon this journey to keep you close to the path, even when you feel you have gone astray.

## Start where you are.

Take stock of your current relational and emotional intimacy—be radically honest with yourself—through this initial appraisal that you will recognise the changes as they occur.

## The Three As

- Acknowledge
- Accept
- Act

During my metaphysical counselling, I was taught the three As. This simple equation has supported me and my clients. You will find it a beneficial tool if you feel stuck, judgmental, or resistant.

## Acknowledge

Assess your current circumstances (this can be applied to all areas of your life). In this case, look at your relationship. Observe what does and what doesn't work for you, within the context of your relationship. What do you love? What leaves you feeling numb or indifferent? What messages did you receive about relationships as a child growing up? Who are your relationship role models? What relationship patterns and messages are you aware of within your friendship circle, family, and the media? What unmet expectations do you currently face in your relationship? Which unmet needs do you have? How do these unmet needs mirror the unmet needs of your childhood? Does your partner remind you of anyone? How could you be showing up differently—why are you not doing this? What do you deeply desire in a relationship with your significant other? How important is this to you? Are you prepared to do the inner work to create what you want to experience? If yes. Great. If not—dig in and be the change you wish to see. You will need a mentor, support, and guidance to assist you in becoming this version of yourself.

We cannot expect to make any meaningful change in our lives if we are not aware of the current lay of the land, and what we are striving for.

If you are working on this with your lover, create separate lists and share them with open hearts—without judgment. You are doing this to understand the other rather than to get your point across.

**Accept:** Sit with your answers to the above prompts.
Once you have acknowledged your current circumstances, it is time to fully accept these wishes, needs, patterns, and unmet aspects within yourself. In this manner, you move out of judgment and resistance to what is and embrace yourself, your needs, and the circumstances of your life—right here as you are, without the desire for it to be different. This is a bold act of love. It is a radical act to sit in the unknown—in the space between what was and what may be—with a wide-open heart full of love.

The patterns you have been living, choosing, and accepting as normal are your experience for a reason. For you, these patterns may be protective mechanisms, or simply due to not knowing any different—or not having a clearer vision for what is possible. There are inherent gifts to be excavated from these previous habits. What did these patterns teach you? What do you know now that you didn't know before? What hidden gifts did these choices afford you? Perhaps you are tenacious, determined, compassionate, courageous, more self-aware, creative, or resilient due to these experiences.

## The path of wholeness.
You may need to do some internal alignment work to help you merge the two separate paths between what was and what you are choosing now. As each pathway leads you towards different outcomes, finding and accepting the gifts inherent within both routes, you may align your actions with what you want to create now. There are many powerful modalities to support this inner work, from NLP, Timeline Therapy, EFT, Past Life Regression, and Energy Psychology integration practices. Avoid only doing talk-based therapies, as our patterns are alive within us and may need a multi-layered approach to transform them. Choose modalities that support you in clearing these energetic patterns—so you may shift with ease and grace into a new energetic frequency and way of being.

**Act:** Shifting the paradigm to make meaningful and lasting change.
Once you have taken the charge out of your current circumstances by fostering an attitude of complete acceptance—you will find yourself naturally ready for a new experience. This is an exciting time of self-discovery and exploration—an adventure in love.

As you explore what you want to develop within your relationship from now on, consciously choose the values you wish to align your actions with, recognise when you come off track and have practices in place to support you in aligning yourself to your current vision.

**Remember:**
Expectations ruin relationships. Let go of the weight of unmet expectations and revel in the beauty of expressing your needs and receiving your lovers' truth—the essence of your connection thrives in these moments of unconditional togetherness.

---

# A VISION OF LOVE FOR YOU

Affirming for a loving and inspiring relationship from the perspective of Metaphysics and the Science of Mind.

*I recognise and acknowledge the Divine Presence, the Infinite Source of all that is. In this sacred moment, I embrace the awareness that this Spiritual Energy is the essence of loving inspiration, and it is ever-present in my life.*

*I now unify my consciousness with the Divine Presence within me. I am one with the Infinite Source of love and divine inspiration. What is true of the Divine is true of me, for I am an individualised expression of this Universal Love.*

*As the Divine contains all qualities and attributes, I understand that I, as the embodiment of the Divine inherently deserve a loving and inspiring relationship. Divine love flows through me effortlessly, igniting my heart and soul with inspiration and filling me with joy.*

*I express profound gratitude for the boundless love and spiritual inspiration within me. I am thankful for the opportunity to experience and share this love with a partner who is equally inspired and passionate about life and our connection.*

*I release any doubts, fears, or limiting beliefs that have hindered my ability to attract and nurture a loving and mutually inspiring relationship. I let go of past experiences that no longer serve my highest good and free myself from all subconscious barriers that have kept me from fully embracing this possibility.*

*I affirm and declare that I am now ready to enter into a loving and inspiring relationship. I radiate love from the depths of my being, attracting a partner who mirrors these qualities. Together, we create a harmonious and loving connection and expand into our fullest potential.*

*I am open to receiving a loving relationship, knowing that the Universe supports my deepest desires. I trust and release these words to the infinite intelligence, knowing it is already done. In deep gratitude and with a heart full of love, I let it be so. And so it is.*

---

# FINAL THOUGHTS

*Love has always been, and will continue to be the answer. Tune into it in the quiet moments—and during those times of immense challenge—let love carry you home to yourself.*

As we embark on this enriching journey of self and relational discovery, we do so for ourselves, for our loved ones and for a greater kindness to humanity itself, knowing that as we thrive and rise with an open heart within the sacred container of our home, collectively, one person, one relationship, one household at a time, we evolve humanity into higher realms of loving acceptance and global awakening, this may seem utopian, but, I believe this is the ripple effect required to shift the paradigm of suffering on the planet—as awakened hearts make better choices beyond the limitations of fear.

This grand vision sings to my heart and speaks truth to me in the small hours, knowing that this is a path for those with courageous hearts—for individuals ready to delve within and undertake the transformative work of self-discovery for the benefit of all. By undertaking this heartfelt task of awakening and becoming the beacon of hope in our homes, supported by our most cherished loved ones, we inspire others to take up the baton of change, too. Someone must go first—is it you? Does your lover join you in this sacred dance of becoming and stand with you upon the threshold of unknown vistas with a wholehearted, full-body YES? If not, show them—you lead—they, inspired, will rise to meet you there as you commit to continually choosing your partner, especially during the most challenging moments.

With immense and soul-searing gratitude, I thank each of you who has adventured in love with me, my beautiful children, my inner circle, and past loves, the teachers I have had the privilege of learning with and the clients I have been honoured to work with. And you, too, for picking up this book and being the change you seek, and I appreciate those whom I have yet to meet.
I love you. You are forever in my heart.

*Charlotte Esmé*

# *What can't be seen can be felt*

What can't be seen can still be felt.

The gentle caress of a lover's thoughts, their desire spanning
aeons of space in a nanosecond.

The receptive moment of stillness as this invisible trail of
fingers on flesh, of the softest kiss upon your soul, awakens
you to a dreamlike awareness of now.

The breeze of their breath sends shockwaves of love across the
imaginal time-space distance of their otherhood.

You, captivated in this moment of unseen togetherness,
breathless, opening to the love that transcends all perceived
separation.

Moved beyond yourself into an unfathomable union of
deepest, truest love.

There need not be more.

What else can there possibly be that is more important than
the engulfing of time and space into absolute reverence of the
here and now?

Love.

Love can't be seen and yet can still be felt.

# Recommended Reading

Books to nourish, guide and support you as you grow beyond your current edges.

Attached by Amir Levine and Rachel S. F. Heller

Dear Lover by David Deida

Feminine Consciousness, Archetypes and Addiction to Perfection by Marion Woodman

Recapture the Rapture: Rethinking God, Sex, and Death in a World That's Lost Its Mind by Jamie Wheal

A Little Book on the Human Shadow by Robert Bly

The Eden Project: In Search of the Magical Other by James Hollis

The Love Poems of Rumi by Nader Khalili

Tantra Illuminated by Christopher D. Wallis

Finding God Through Sex by David Deida

The Radiance Sutras by Lorin Roche

A Return to Love by Marianne Williamson

Ancestral Medicine by Daniel Foor

Walking The Tiger by Peter A. Levine

When the Body Says No by Babor Mate

The Alchemist by Paulo Coelo

The Power of Vulnerability by Brené Brown

Becoming Supernatural: How Common People Are Doing the Uncommon by Adam Boyce, Joe Dispenza

In Sync with the Opposite Sex: Understand the Conflicts, End the Confusion, Make the Right Choices by Alison A. Armstrong

Women Who Run With The Wolves by Clarissa Pinkola Estés

Taoist Yoga and Sexual Energy Transforming Your Body, Mind, and Spirit by Eric Steven Yudelove

Healing Love Through the Tao by Mantak Chia and Maneewan Chia

Stealing Fire by Jamie Wheal and Steven Kotler

Tantra the Path of Ecstasy by Georg Feuerstein

## About Charlotte

Charlotte is passionate about supporting her clients in aligning with love, with their hearts courageously open and free.

Charlotte believes that if we, as couples, honour the sacredness of our union, choose to work on ourselves, and deepen our capacity for intimacy, connection, and individual growth, our relationships will thrive, and our family will be nourished by our continued and deepening connection. Charlotte believes that if individuals, couples, and families grow beyond our habitual patterns and edges of closure, fear, and withholding, we will recognise that Heaven on Earth exists right here within our own home.

This connection radiates outwards to nourish our friends, family, and communities. As we each take radical responsibility for how we show up, our consciousness expands exponentially as we shift into a paradigm of unity, mutual love, respect, and infinite possibility. In connecting to the sacredness in all and within every circumstance, we create change and evolve beyond our limitations together.

Charlotte's approach is steeped in two decades of experience studying metaphysics and many personal development modalities, and guiding, mentoring and supporting clients through challenging times and expanding into their next-level vision as they embody their dream lives. Work privately, by application only, with Charlotte through her one-on-one mentoring or during a private bespoke retreat.

You will most likely find Charlotte exploring wildscapes, in the forest, walking barefoot on the sand of a beautiful beach, dancing in the moonlight, hanging out with her family, oil painting, writing poetry, enjoying the opera, or eating cake and sipping strong black coffee in a local café.

# A ROMANTIC GETAWAY TO A SECLUDED LOVE NEST

*You cannot decide what you deeply desire—it erupts through you, entices you, and pulls at your heartstrings.*

Imagine leaving behind the hustle and bustle of everyday life, hand in hand with your loved one, to embark on a breathtaking journey to a location untouched by the chaos of the outside world. You venture far away from your daily routine, ascending into the heart of the mountains, where tranquillity and serenity meet you at every turn. The winding and hair-raising mountain passes only add to the sense of adventure, making every twist and turn an exhilarating shared thrill. With each mile passed, your anticipation grows, knowing that a haven of love and intimacy awaits you.

Finally, you arrive at your secluded cabin, perched high in the mountains, with its rustic charm and cosy elegance embracing you like an old friend. You find it nestled amidst the wilderness, feeling like a hidden treasure, a secret shared only by you and your beloved. The crisp, invigorating air and the snowflakes that float from the heavens create a soft, loving blanket of peace around you.

Outside, the world transforms into a magical winter wonderland, where trees bow gracefully under their snowy burden. The beauty of the natural world fills your heart with a sense of wonder and appreciation—it is as though the mountains themselves whisper their secrets of love, serenity, and connection to you.

A welcoming log fire crackles inside the cabin, casting a warm and inviting glow. The soft flicker of candlelight dances playfully, setting the mood for an enchanting week ahead. Thick and plush rugs adorn the wooden floors, beckoning you to kick off your shoes and sink into their embrace. The cupboards are generously stocked with an array of delicious foods, each chosen to delight your senses. The aroma of fresh coffee wafts from the stove, promising cosy mornings spent snuggled in with your beloved.

As the evening draws near, a bottle of wine patiently awaits you to uncork it. The anticipation of the night ahead fills the room with a subtle excitement and longing. You know that in this idyllic setting, every moment will be a chance to deepen your connection, explore the depths of your love, and create memories that will last a lifetime.

You may prefer a different location, perhaps perched on a cliff overlooking a wild and crashing sea, with waves sending their salty spray high into the air, catching the light of the setting sun, whilst the sound of the ocean rhythm becomes a sensual symphony, a backdrop for your own love story.

From the secluded love nest, whether amidst the serene snow-cloaked mountains or by the tempestuous sea—the world of familiarity and habit fades away. It's just the two of you, bound by love, desire, and the promise of unforgettable moments together as you dive deep into the practices in this book. Your senses are awakened, your hearts are entwined, and as you look into each other's eyes, you know that this is a moment you'll cherish forever.

# OTHER PUBLICATIONS BY CHARLOTTE ESMÉ

Love and Grace Sacred Poems and Prayers

Yoga Through the Seasons

Awakening WILD Shadow Alchemy

Living the Chakras

Archetypes: Live an Empowered Life

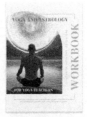

Yoga and Astrology

Charlotte Esmé  Author Page
https://www.amazon.co.uk/stores/author/B0BSLQFHC4

Printed in Great Britain
by Amazon

33940255R00066